NAPOLEON HILL CERTIFIED INSTRUCTORS & STUDENTS

And TOM "TOO TALL" CUNNINGHAM PRESENTS...

GOING THE
EXTRA MILE

GOING THE
EXTRA MILE

Table of Contents

Dedication

"If I had to choose but one of the seventeen principles of success and rest my chances on that principle alone, I would, without hesitation, choose going the extra mile, because this is the principle through which one can make himself indispensable to others."

— Napoleon Hill

"They who give time, or money, or shelter, to the stranger...do, as it were, put God under obligation to them, so perfect are the compensations of the universe."

— Ralph Waldo Emerson

This book is dedicated to those of you who go the extra mile in every area of your life. Now more than ever, going the extra mile at whatever job you have, or business you own, is certain to bring you financial success and personal satisfaction. *Going The Extra Mile* in your personal life as a spouse, parent, and community member will bring you love, respect, and fulfillment, and create a better future for all of us.

Tom too tall Cunningham

Napoleon Hill Certified Instructor

Creator of the Journeys To Success book series

Acknowledgements

Initially, I thank God for the opportunity to share an experience of my life in this book, which is intended to inspire readers to be even better people.

Much gratitude goes to the Napoleon Hill Foundation for the excellent work of enhancing "The Law of Success" throughout the world.

A big thank-you to the creators of this project; Mr. Brad Szollose, the creative cover designer of this book and Mr. John Westley Clayton our Publisher for the many hours he put into this project to bring this work to fruition.

My thanks to Mr. Tom Cunningham who idealized this book. He is a professional who puts ideas into practice.

I ask God to always take care of my homeland, my family and everyone who is focused on making Napoleon Hill's Philosophy a reality everywhere on this planet.

Foreword

I can never repay Napoleon Hill for how he has contributed to my life.

I consider myself to be a pretty tough fellow and I have survived a lot but sitting in a hospital with a methicillin-resistant Staphylococcus aureus, a very nasty staph infection that almost took my life, was the feat that took the most mental strength to defeat - I literally got to the point that I had no heartbeat and was fortunate to be revived by CPR.

Apparently I got an infection by scraping my forearm when I tripped over an electric cord hooked up to my Tesla electric car in my garage. Who would have ever thought that small fall would be something that would almost kill me?

I spent about seven months in that hospital recovering from near death and whenever I felt like giving up I would tell myself,

"That makes you the worst kind of hypocrite. If you give up now, you will wash away forty years of delivering speeches to tens of thousands of people, encouraging them to never give up, to deal with whatever obstacles have been put in their way, to find the courage to face those obstacles head on! Screw it. I won't quit. Not now, not ever!"

If that man didn't bring me back from death, I wouldn't even be here writing to you. So I want to choose the most powerful words that I can to share with you next.

First of all, each chapter of this book has been contributed by a student or instructor of Napoleon Hill's philosophy. And each word that has been contributed can be exactly what you need to hear to get over that obstacle currently in your way.

But my biggest piece of advice to you is to study and get to know the 17 Principles of Success because they will give you the roadmap to all the success you can ever imagine. This book is about just one of the principles so make it a commitment to study the rest.

After struggling financially for the first decade after starting the RE/MAX franchise in 1973, I've became extraordinary wealthy. But who would have ever guessed that I would go from milking cows to starting a multi-billion-dollar real estate company?

Look, I was 27 years old when I started RE/MAX. I didn't know what I was doing. I had no game plan. I didn't know how to run a business or manage people. It wasn't just our competitors trying to put us out of business. We were doing a pretty good job of that ourselves.

What I did do was GO THE EXTRA MILE.

I read every book I could get my hands on about motivating people and how great companies, like McDonalds were created, underlining passages that spoke to me. I attended seminars offered by Disney. I made fun of companies like Herbalife, Amway and Mary Kay, but attended their conferences to see what lessons could be learned that would be relevant to making RE/MAX better.

It goes without saying; I worked hard. I still do.

I've done a lot in life. I have been a father. I've adventured. I've owned a NASCAR racing team, gone deep-sea diving all over the world, (including exploring a Japanese ship wreck from World War II in the South Pacific), skydived from airplanes and hot-air balloons, have a jet-pilot license and bagged big-game while hunting in Africa.

And I know that if you continue to be a student of Napoleon Hill's work, you too will be able to say that you have done everything in life that you wanted to do.

Sincerely,

Dave Liniger

Co-Founder of RE/MAX

Introduction

When we come across motivational and inspirational life stories, we often find that *Going the Extra Mile* had something to do with them. Stories about overcoming challenges and accomplishing great feats usually stem from this principle.

Going the Extra Mile is filled with incredible stories written by Napoleon Hill Foundation Certified Instructors and Students. The authors write about the goals they have achieved and the challenges they have encountered in their lives and how *Going The Extra Mile* was the difference maker for them.

The goal of this book is to use the principle of "*Going the Extra Mile*" to inspire you to take the initiative to pursue your purpose with passion. It takes persistence, effort, and dedication before you receive a return on your investment and achieve your goal and we hope this book will be an encouragement to you.

Going The Extra Mile teaches us that we have to give in order to get, we have to strive in order to grow, and we have to believe in a life with no limitations to achieve the incredible.

It is the difference maker that will give you the competitive advantage over life's opportunities and challenges.

— Stella Tartsinis

At this time you have in your hands not a common book, but a collection of experiences and precepts shared by business leaders and prominent instructors, lecturers, public speakers, mentors and coaches from around the world certified by the Napoleon Hill Foundation. This copy shall be our best guide where we can find answers to strategize and overcome barriers that threaten the virtual conquest of some goal or realize a project.

Perhaps in the past we have investigated in one and another recipe without achieving effective results, looking for those secrets that lead us to achieve our goals, or perhaps we have attended seminars that in that moment help us on racing the fighting spirit and ignite engines of our initiative, but even after we take some action fails to go beyond being another failed attempt and we wonder hard or even stopped believing in our ability.

The fact is that to recover from these failed searches on motivational books that give us excuses to argue a comfortable explanation of why we abandon some established purpose, then here we provide detailed reasons why perhaps we have not reached such purposes, knowing that there are tools at our disposal to embrace success.

The proposal here is that we let ourselves be conquered by the stories and precepts here embodied and search on each of them for any key, perhaps a secret or track, a principle, a law, some inspiration, something that makes us move the internal will and lead us to what we want to achieve. Thus, with determination and commitment that here we acquire, we are confident that in the process we will improve all these qualities we already have, discovering that we did not know we have and realizing each story below is impregnated with experiences, whose common denominator at the end the day is Success or the conquest of dreams that seemed so distant and impossible. In advance we should thank ourselves for having taken the time to scrutinize this guide accepting that there is always a new opportunity to transform effectively and stay alert to change course when necessary, always embracing Success.

— Francisco Mendoza

Distinguido Lector, en este momento tiene usted en sus manos no un libro común, sino una recopilación de experiencias y preceptos compartidos por grandes empresarios y destacados instructores, conferencistas, mentores y entrenadores de distintas partes del mundo certificados por la Fundación Napoleon Hill. Este ejemplar deberá ser nuestra mejor guía donde podremos consultar las respuestas para elaborar estrategias y rebasar los obstáculos que amenazan la virtual conquista de alguna meta o concretar un proyecto.

Tal vez en el pasado hemos indagado en una y otra receta sin lograr resultados efectivos, buscando esos secretos que nos lleven a lograr lo que tanto queremos, o tal vez asistimos a seminarios que en su momento nos prometen elevar el espíritu de lucha y encender los motores de nuestra iniciativa, pero aun después de que tomamos un poco de acción no pasa de ir más allá de ser otro intento fallido y nos cuestionamos duramente o hasta dejamos de creer en nuestra capacidad…

El caso es, que para recuperarnos de esas fallidas búsquedas en libros motivacionales que nos dan excusas para argumentar una cómoda explicación del porqué abandonamos algún propósito establecido, entonces aquí podemos proporcionar detalladamente razones por las cuales tal vez no hemos alcanzado tales propósitos, estando nosotros seguros de que hay herramientas a nuestra disposición para abrazar el éxito.

La propuesta aquí es que nos dejemos conquistar por las historias y los preceptos aquí plasmados y busquemos en cada uno de ellos alguna clave, una llave, tal vez un secreto, una pista, un principio, una ley, alguna inspiración, o algo que nos haga mover la voluntad interna y nos impulse hacia lo que queremos lograr. Así, con la determinación y compromiso que aquí adquirimos, estamos seguros de que en el proceso mejoraremos todas esas cualidades que ya tenemos , descubriendo las que no sabíamos que poseemos y percatándonos que cada historia a continuación viene impregnada de experiencias, cuyo común denominador al final del día es el Éxito o la conquista de sueños que parecían tan lejanos e imposibles. Por adelantado debemos agradecernos a nosotros mismos por habernos tomado el tiempo de escudriñar esta guía y aceptar que siempre hay una nueva oportunidad para transformarnos efectivamente y mantenernos alertas para cambiar el rumbo cuando sea necesario, abrazando siempre el Éxito.

— Francisco Mendoza

CHAPTER 1

It Was All For The Best

By Tamara Tillman

Imagine yourself in a picture of an autumn morning, in about early November, with foliage and fresh cool air, perhaps somewhere in Europe. Into this picture enters a young woman full of vigor refreshed by a morning shower. She is dressed in scrubs ready for a long workday in an operating room. The woman is stepping into an elegant gray car, starting the engine and driving to work. At 6 AM every city wakes up to its own pace; some get up slowly to forgiving town streets, with ordinary people, among them those who like to leave home a bit early to get ahead of the traffic. Still, there are other people who prefer to read a newspaper with their coffee. There are yet others who are surfing laptop screens, while the early birds have arrived at work. Amidst an urban morning, like many others, our gray car is traveling by the old railway station through a shortcut street known only to locals. This side road may save 20 minutes, and in our story, it may even save a life (spoiler alert).

In the gray car that makes its way, like any other day, toward a peripheral hospital located 40 minutes away from home, the driver is I, an accomplished physician who has been able to realize her youthful dream of establishing a skin-cancer center. This was a dream inspired by the loss of my mother to Melanoma some two decades before. To honor my mother's memory, instead of daily grieving, with whom I could not share the experience of my first and last love, who has neither seen me graduate from Surgery residency, nor buy my first home, nor partake in other of my life's celebrations, I decided to establish a cancer center. Every morning when practicing medicine at the skin-cancer center, I remembered my mother. She was a good, beautiful woman, who loved

1

the ambiance of laughing people and who appreciated the small pleasures in life. It might have been the 4 o'clock coffee, or chatting with one of her endless number of friends at the neighborhood café or, the impeccably dressed lady like who looked like a movie star. With her blond hair and her blue-green eyes, she looked like Ingrid Bergman. Hers was a huge love for outdoor activities, basking in the sun, the sand on the seashore, pure freedom.

To me every morning had been a replay of my biggest mission in life. My job was to care for other mothers (and fathers) so that they live to see their daughters grow to become independent, start families and hunt for mortgages. This privilege was not bestowed on my mom.

Driving early mornings through the neglected alleys around the railway station with its single traffic light was a hidden gem. Perhaps it did not offer the best views, but surely it was the shortest way. That lonely traffic light did not always operate; often it would just flicker. On this morning traffic is even better than expected, so I think this means that the traffic light is working. Sweet! So, when my gray car arrived at the green light, barely beginning to negotiate the junction, the moment of sweet serenity is suddenly shattered by another car that has failed to yield to its own red light.

At the moment of impact, I am jolted to and fro in my seat, coming finally to a rest by colliding with the steering wheel. Thank God for the seatbelt, I think while flying back and forth in the car compartment. After the initial shock, when I realize that my car is probably a total loss, I call my older brother. To my good fortune all my family lived at the time no more than a few blocks from each other, and so we can always help one another on short notice. He is still at home-- what a relief! "Can you please pick me up?" I ask him, "it looks as if my vehicle has been damaged and I must arrive at work quickly because I have five patients waiting in the OR". "Certainly" is the answer from the other side of the mobile phone, and he adds: "Did you call Mike yet?" I am not sure that I understand the question well, so after a brief silence I reply, "Who the heck is Mike?" At that point, I think I hear him smile on the other end. "He is your hubby. Don't you move anywhere until I and or your husband or the police arrive".

At the nearby ER, between x-rays and examinations I started to reflect upon the crash. My head had bounced back and forth in that accident in much the same way as that of Cam Newton the Carolina Panthers quarterback when he smashed into another NFL player. Both

☐
☐
☐
☐
☐
☐
☐
☐
☐
☐
☐
☐
☐

"Great things
are done by a series of
small things brought together."

—VINCENT VAN GOGH

he and I will need to be on a concussion protocol for a week or two. In medical schools, there is a compelling concussion simulation with a red jelly in a clear glass ball. The biomechanical forces after such a hit result in spinning, oscillation and even stretching of that poor jelly. No wonder my mind is bleary. I am starting to get dizzy, my head is sore and my left arm has tingles. Now I think to myself: "calm down, my dear, no stress now", with my background disease of blood clotting for which stress can be a trigger, I may end up with a more dangerous condition than the car crash I just experienced. Finally, I was discharged from the ER with instructions to rest for a week.

That was a prolonged aching and painful week and, after promising not to over-work, I returned to my cancer center just to witness a backlog of patients.

"Gee, I love this place", I thought to myself when I stepped into the Operating Rooms. The combination of clean smell, cold air, and holy work are addicting. It can be very cool in an operating room. This is something I have learned over the years: if the entire staff of doctors, nurses and the technician are made up of males, I am doomed to freeze for the rest of that day. Boys appear to need a very low temperature to function. Today was my lucky day with only women staff meaning it is going to be a warm and gossipy day at the OR. A blond, brilliant, woman full of life and the giggling technician were already waiting at the OR. When I initially started working at the hospital and created the new cancer center, Ida volunteered to help me and became the lab master. Motivated only by her own love of work she was the first to volunteer to work with me. She was a quick learner and a real curious person. Soon she was controlling the technique and within no time starting to teach me new tricks. I loved that creative and dedicated girl. She became my colleague and my inspiration on how to learn new things and master them. "How are you doing today, Doc?" she asked. "You know," I reply, "a classical whiplash. A little sore head, some nausea and the left hand not quite right, but it is by the book, don't worry."

We started with the first skin cancer patient. This was one of the physicians in the hospital who as a child underwent skull radiation for another disease, resulting in multiple skin lesions as an adult. He was one of our "frequent flyers". We had already reconstructed his left cheek and left forehead this year. Now it was time for his ear. The ear cartilage is not a forgiving organ, and any lesion that is attached to the cartilage is both hard to excise and hard to reconstruct. It is challenging but gratifying once it is done. As I worked on this patient I started to feel uncomfortable with grasping the stainless-steel instruments; nothing specific, just not my regular grip. Ida was all over; she was taking the skin cancer specimens to the lab next door where she cut and dyed them, creating a cancer map. Then we returned to the OR to cut another layer of skin cancer until the patient was cancer free. This was a long but rewarding process that often takes hours.

The next patient was a new one, a middle-aged female with a huge lesion beneath her right lower eyelid, already distorting the lid. After the local anesthesia, I drew on the patient the cancer borders and started to cut with a hefty margin. I lost my left-hand grip and my balance with the last cut of the eyelid specimen. The forceps fell on the floor, leaving no doubt as to the severity of my condition. We canceled the rest of the operations that day, and I was rushed to take a CT scan of my neck and my spine. As the radiology assistant showed me the locker room and I changed my scrub clothing, Ida came running and burst into the radiology center. "Stop everything," she said. "Dr. Tilleman has been trying for years to get pregnant, so let's make sure she is not actually pregnant now before exposing her." My dear Ida took a blood sample while I was on the X-ray table. To make a long story short, that blood test came back positive and the CT tests were canceled.

The accident I was involved in marked the end of my surgical career.

I was diagnosed with limbs disability that needed years of rehabilitation. But every cloud has a silver lining. That very same devastating accident enabled my husband and I to become parents. Remember my coagulation disorder? Since all my previous pregnancies were not detected early enough, I had developed blood clots, which resulted in many miscarriages. This time, because of the accident, we found out very early that I was pregnant so I was able to inject anticoagulated drugs to prevent micro-coagulation and miscarriage.

That accident saved the fetus that is now our wonderful daughter, Daphne. Because of the accident and because of Ida our lab technician who literally went that extra mile to save our fetus from irreversible radiation effects, we would soon be embracing our child.

Tamara Tillman | Bio

Dr. Tilleman is a Surgeon and a Dean of medical school who has devoted considerable research to paradigms and how they affect personal and organizational success.

Dr. Tilleman has shown that the key to gaining more freedom and to living life to the fullest is revealing and eradicating your private paradigms. Her research yielded over 80 publications and a clear conclusion regarding the essential skills to produce successful and lasting change.

Per her studies, people view the world through a paradigm filter where reality is heavily influenced by subjective interpretations of daily events. Paradigms will replace the reality to the extent that most people feel confident that their interpretation is the only objective reality.

Her two innovative training programs: "Successier" ™ and "Leadership without Paradigms" ™ are based on her Paradigm Research at Harvard University, Maastricht University, and Erasmus University.

Dr. Tilleman can be reached at tamaratilleman.com or 212-505-0055

CHAPTER 2

The Impostor Syndrome

By Walter Kaltenbach

One of the biggest barriers that prevent people from getting out of their comfort zone is when they fear they are weeds rooted in society. They firmly believe they are not qualified for the position they have and that their life achievements have come by chance or luck. It is a fear that strikes many people; the impostor syndrome.

Even I, who have been training and lecturing thousands of people, have come across thoughts like:

Am I the right person to talk about such a profound subject to this audience?

At the end of my presentation, will the audience be glad that they invested their time listening to me?

This is only a personal example and I think you, the reader of this chapter, have your own examples and have also felt weak in the knees, questioning whether you were the right person for the situation.

I am glad to know that I'm not the only one! What can you and I do to overcome these feelings of inadequacy that so many of us experience?

This is exactly the point of this article. It will help us to understand what Socrates was talking about in ancient Greece when he said; "Know thyself".

The term 'Impostor Syndrome' was first coined in an article published in 1978 by two clinical psychologists named Dr. Pauline R. Clance and Dr. Suzanne Imes. They pointed out that the syndrome strikes accomplished and highly successful individuals who are marked by the inability to internalize their achievements and by the persistent fear of being exposed as a "fraud".

Despite all the external evidence of their competence, people with this syndrome remain convinced that they are a fake and do not deserve the success they have achieved. They think and believe that their success is the result of sheer luck or timely chance. An impostor even believes that his peers find him more intelligent and competent than he thinks he is.

Some scientific studies suggest that the impostor syndrome is particularly common among high performance women who think they are inferior in the male-dominated corporate world. Other studies show that men also face this syndrome in their daily lives due to the competitive world. We can say that "human beings" like you and I face it somehow. It is estimated that two out of five successful people consider themselves as frauds. Other studies have found that 70 percent of all people feel like impostors at some point in their lives.

The impostor syndrome is studied and understood more as a reaction to certain stimuli and events. It is not perceived as a mental disorder but has been the subject of research by many psychologists. Although traditionally understood as a rooted personality trait, it is a response experienced by many different people and in situations that ask for such feelings. It is true that some people experience it more intensely than others in different situations. Nonetheless, it is real and we must face it.

What Napoleon Hill realized in his previous works of the contemporary term, and published in the *Law of Success* is that all people have fears. We must learn to understand and face them. When you are paralyzed by and cannot take action then you are not tested and therefore you do not get a result, either positive or negative. But, when we confront our fears, we get out of our comfort zone and produce above average results.

I remember a very profound experience I had in 1992 when I was 17 years old back. At that time, I was a youth group member of a Rotary International Interact Club. I always believed that ecology is paramount for the planet and I had developed a project to plant 1 million trees in Sao Paulo City, Brazil. That project of mine was embraced by the city municipality.

In that year, Brazil hosted the first United Nations Conference on Environment and Development, held between June 3 – 14, 1992 in the city of Rio de Janeiro. The event, which became known as ECO-92 or Rio-92, evaluated existing problems and progress made in the world regarding ecology. Important documents were produced and they remain as reference guidelines for environmental discussions about the planet.

Unlike the Stockholm Conference, Eco-92 was special because of the presence of numerous heads of state, clearly demonstrating the relevance of environmental issues in the early 1990's.

My project was selected to be presented at this event and I, as the creator of it, was chosen to make the oral presentation in loco. I was thrilled with the opportunity because I have always been driven by challenges. Today, I realize that I had no idea of the greatness of the opportunity and what I would face while preparing for it. When I got home, and told my mother about it, she panicked! She knew that being the official ECO 92 presenter of the project in that international event was an immense responsibility for a 17-year-old student to take on. She grabbed me by the hand and we did a thorough preparation of all the text that I would speak and all the visuals I would use with the use of the old slide carousel, which projects negatives of slides onto a big screen. She had a VHS video camera and we would record my presentation so I could train and watch the recording in my room and discuss what could be improved. We would immediately record, watch and revise it again. We did it several times and for several days until the big day.

I got up early, put on my new suit, purchased specifically for the occasion, and went to the airport to catch the one-hour flight to Rio de Janeiro. When I landed, I came across the actual size, magnitude and international impact of the event. I remember that I was weak in the knees and really nervous, because I realized I had been too naive, even negligent, for not wanting to rationalize that this event was in fact grandiose in its international importance.

The positive side was that we arrived almost at the last minute of my presentation and I did not have enough time to be mulling it over until they called me on stage with thousands of people looking at me. At that time, I felt an impostor. What was I doing? Weren't there better prepared people for this? Would the world listen to a 17-year-old?

I had no answer. I could only take action and do what I had trained with my mother. There were thousands of people staring at me. I know I did my best and I became a giant; speaking properly, putting my soul, strength, momentum, joy and love for the cause I was defending. I completed believed in the project and it showed in my presentation.

When I finished, to my surprise, I received a standing ovation. I left with a feeling that I had grown many years and acquired maturity for having grabbed the opportunity life had given me. And I did not count on luck but on preparation to do my best. I could not have done better because I just did my best. Those cheers were just the result of preparatory work and conviction, believing in a purpose. It was the proof that going the extra mile is worthwhile

At that point I knew I was not an impostor, that I had expressed credibility to others and for this reason I had been the chosen one. And with the reputation given to me I learned to respect and understand that an impostor comes alive when we do not prepare ourselves so that we deceive others and ourselves. That was not my case at all.

Now that I have given an account of a story of my life, I have a question for you readers:

Were the people who have experienced the Impostor Syndrome inside or outside their Comfort Zone?

They were outside of their comfort zone of course! Because, if they were inside, they would not have experienced the situation and questioned whether the applause and recognition was real, factual and worthy of praise.

What did those people do then?

They prepared themselves by studying and working hard in order to prevent people from finding out they were "impostors". This hard work often leads to more praise and success. What perpetuates the feelings of being an impostor is the fear of being "caught". The impostor may feel they need to work two or three times as hard and more intensely than others. When they least expect it, they have become the reference in what they do. That is, they may even think they are impostors but in fact, they are not. The more they demand from themselves, the harder they study and work, the more success they will have! By doing that they are applying *Napoleon Hill's Success Principle* of *Going The Extra Mile*.

Summarizing my dear reader, let the Impostor Syndrome come to us all so that we can just show that the "farce" is just a reason for us to "Go The Extra Mile" and by doing that we will stand out in our field.

Some people might say that the Impostor Syndrome is just a tall tale to entertain children and live life with a more interesting storyline.

I am sure that soon we will find ourselves at the top if we always Go The Extra Mile.

Walter Kaltenbach | Bio

Walter Kaltenbach is a Brazilian with German citizenship, currently living in Sao Paulo, Brazil. He is the Head of Master Mind Training for the Napoleon Hill Foundation licensee in Brazil and other Portuguese-speaking countries.

He is a business administrator, economist, master of customer service and people management, and a Napoleon Hill Foundation Certified Instructor.

Walter graduated from the School of Business and the Business Institute of Albuquerque in the areas of communication, interpersonal intelligence, leadership, sales and management. His training courses and lectures have been attended by over 25.000 executives, professionals and students who want to excel in their area of expertise.

He has been a motivational speaker for more than 20 years and the author of the book The Law of Success in the 21st Century.

Walter can be reached at........

e-mail: walterka@uol.com.br,

Skype: Walter Kaltenbach

Phone: 55 11 98542-5057

Facebook: Walter Kaltenbach

Address: Rua Jaragua, 737 – apto: 257 Cores - CEP: 01129-000 – São Paulo – SP - Brazil

CHAPTER 3

Compensation

By Elyse Hargreaves

If I could put my money on any of the 17 Principles, which would give you the greatest benefits, without hesitation I would say *Going the Extra Mile*. Napoleon Hill himself said something very similar, but why?

To understand the principle of *Going the Extra Mile*, you first need to understand the law of nature, which is behind it. This "*Law of Nature*" was first commented on by Isaac Newton in his revolutionary masterpiece: Philosophiæ Naturalis Principia Mathematica (Mathematical Principles of Natural Philosophy) which was first published in 1687. In this scientific book, Newton showed that: three laws of motion, combined with his law of universal gravitation, explained Kepler's laws of planetary motion. It is the third law, which is most relevant to our topic, namely:

Law III: To every action there is always opposed an equal reaction.

Another way to understand this concept of give and take, is by the use of another law of nature:

The Law of conservation of energy: Energy can neither be created nor destroyed; rather, it transforms from one form to another.

This law is known as the First Law of Thermodynamics and is used in physics very often. The most interesting thing about this law is that when energy transforms from one form to another, the total amount of energy is never changed. For instance, chemical energy can be converted to kinetic energy in the explosion of a stick of dynamite, yet the quantity of the potential chemical energy (when converted to kinetic energy) remains the same. The only thing that has changed in regards to the energy is its quality, not its quantity. There is an equal amount of give and take; the pendulum swings forward as much as it swings back.

There is a kind of balance in nature, and this applies to everything within our Cosmos, including you and I. But how can we apply this to our daily lives, how does it even affect our daily lives?

The best way to understand how this law of nature applies to us is using a simple word called 'Compensation'. There have been many great thinkers in our past who have commented extensively on this term. Ralph Waldo Emerson was one of the most recent men of this type, and wrote an exquisite essay on Compensation. However, that was many years ago and the world seems very different to how it was in the late nineteenth century. The question is, how does it apply to us today?

In many religions, it is taught that your compensation will come to you in the next life. If you do well now, you can go to heaven; do bad now, and you must be punished and go to hell. This is your 'compensation', and it comes to you from a world other than our own, a place we know nothing about. Sound familiar? The poor shall inherit good fortune in heaven, and those with good fortune now will have it taken from them. But this does not make any sense, why is it bad to have good fortune? Why is it good to be poor?

With wisdom, we can understand what the real essence of fortune is. Money is neither good nor evil. Rather, it is just a piece of paper (or plastic), with only a perception of value. It is a tool we use to exchange values. The true good (or bad) that comes from a tool is the way it is used. Is a knife good or evil? You can use a knife to cook a beautiful dinner for your family, or you can use that same knife to murder or cause harm. It is the way in which it is used which gives the knife its power, not the mere possession of it.

The same holds true for money; it is neither evil nor good. It all depends on who is holding the tool. How then, can others preach that money is evil? This kind of understanding of 'compensation' is shaky, it does not hold up to our criticisms and questions. It is full of holes and quite frankly, a bit confusing. It takes 'compensation' and turns it into something 'supernatural', something which we can't understand or is out of our control. This type of understanding is not accurate, and therefore it is not in our best interest to hold as our own truism.

Compensation is a part of nature, therefore it is something that happens in this life, not the next. Compensation, as I have tried to explain using the laws of physics, is a natural part of our cosmos, and a natural part of our lives. It always has been and always will be a natural law, which affects every single individual. It does not discriminate depending on your background or education. If you walk over the edge of a high-rise building, gravity will cause you to fall whether you believe in it or not. Just as you cannot turn on and off the laws of physics, which determine that you will fall, you cannot evade or go around the law of Compensation.

There is only one formula in the whole Philosophy of Individual Achievement by Napoleon Hill. If you truly understand this formula, it will not only help you to make sense of the world, but it will guide you in this life much more effectively than other formulas you may have learned in the past. Why this formula is not taught in school, yet we learn Euclidean geometry (which is not really used unless you are a mathematician), is a wonder to me. Here it is:

Quality + Quantity + Mental Attitude =
Compensation ($+Responsibility)

Now it is important to understand that Compensation in this formula can mean anything, it can come in many different forms. However, the most common and easiest to understand for this discussion is the Compensation of material gain. It is very important to remember that money and responsibility go hand in hand, you cannot have increased pay without increased responsibility. Money has a lot of potential power and with great power comes great responsibility. Ask Spiderman; he knows that.

Many celebrities get compensated with a lot of money, though is it not interesting that they are not taught that responsibility comes with it? Like most of us, they would prefer not to have it. Without responsibility, you can do whatever you want, say whatever you want, and not have to worry about the consequences. But this is not the way Compensation works. You cannot increase your material wealth without increasing your responsibility.

Why do celebrities get compensated so much? Most of the time, it seems that they do not have to work very hard for it. Can we make sense of it by using the Q + Q + MA formula? Success multiplies and gets easier and easier as time goes on, because with increased success comes increased recognition. If more people know about your product, then you do not have to try so hard to sell it.

Pop music is a classic example, and the easiest to use. Please do not misunderstand me here, I respect other people's profession, and I am not here to talk about my opinions. I am merely stating some obvious points, which will help you to understand the nature of Compensation. For this example, I would like to use Britney Spears as she is someone familiar to us all. There is one song I would like to use as my example, it is a collaborative song called 'Scream & Shout' by will.i.am featuring Britney Spears. Fortunately, you do not need to know this song to understand the example I am sharing. Brittney does not have much to feature in this song; in fact, she only sings one or two lines. These lines would have taken less than a minute to say, and a button needed to be pressed to have it repeated throughout the song. How much would you say Britney Spears was compensated for this song?

Quite a lot; thousands, hundreds of thousands; perhaps millions. Why? How can it be that she can say one line, specifically: "Britney B#T*H" and be paid so much for it? The answer lies in the Q + Q + MA formula. As I said, this is a formula that applies to everyone, whether you're a normal Joe walking down the street or your "Britney B#T*H".

The work that she put into this song was of lesser quality than perhaps her other music. In other songs, she has a lot more involvement; in this song she has hardly any involvement at all. This 'involvement' can be considered the quality of what she puts into the song. The Quality is low, but there is something that is VERY high…. Can you guess what it is? That's right, the Quantity! If the Quantity is very high, you can have a very low quality, and still be compensated with millions. If we were to replace the Q + Q + MA formula with numbers, we could describe Britney's Compensation like this:

10 (Low Quality) + 20 million (Quantity) + Positive Attitude (Mental Attitude) = 2 million dollars + Responsibility

Mass production can sometimes produce products, which are of a lower quality because SO many people buy it. That is why a low-quality product like McDonalds has such a high profit margin, because everyone eats it. The quality does not have to be high to receive high compensation. This is a simple business rule, supply and demand.

This law of Compensation is not good or evil; it is just the way it is. If someone falls off a building and dies, you would not say that nature killed them; they simply did not relate themselves properly to the laws of nature. The only scary thing about it is how little the world understands of it. Because of this little understanding, we justify producing low quality mass production because it still pays a lot of money. If only we could all see the value in putting principle above the dollar, quality above quantity.

Erwin Schrödinger was a Nobel Prize-winning Austrian physicist who developed a number of fundamental results in the field of quantum theory, which formed the basis of wave mechanics. In October 1956 he delivered a series of lectures at Trinity College in Cambridge. The topics were Mind and Matter, and these lectures can be found in his book with this same title. I would like to quote a sentence he used when discussing the dangers to intellectual evolution:

"Now I believe that the increasing mechanization and 'stupidization' of most manufacturing processes involve serious danger of a general degeneration of our organ of intelligence."

Granted, he was referring to the assembly line, which was becoming highly optimized during that time, but I think that this is just as relevant to our discussion as it was to his. Whatever you don't use, you lose. Take one of your arms and strap it to your side and after a while it will begin to entropy and waste away. Our brain is as much an organ as our lungs or heart, we need to use it for it to continue to function the way it should. We may be at risk of losing the greatest asset we have been given through Evolution by Natural Selection, the power of the human mind.

How did it become like this? Why is it that some areas of our pop culture do not have a high quality, yet have such a high quantity? "Next to want, boredom has become the worst scourge in our lives." (Erwin Schrödinger – Mind and Matter)

The answer is, we are bored. No one knows what to do with their time and they think the answer is on the couch, at the corner bar or the fast food drive through. Evolution has taken us to a pinnacle, the likes we have never seen before anywhere in the cosmos. The human mind is the most complex and amazing tool, which every human is given at birth. This tool has allowed us the advantage of moving beyond the struggle of survival. All other animals, which are limited in their availability of expression, are much more focused on survival. We, on the other hand, are at the top of the food chain. We have used our intelligence to make tools, which aid us tremendously in giving us more spare time.

The problem is that no one knows how they want to spend the majority of that time. Ask someone what they want out of life, and they will most likely say: to be happy. What is the problem with that answer? It is not very specific. You cannot be so vague with what you want, because you will produce the same vagueness in your outcome. When you are aiming for a three-point shot in basketball, you must aim in one spot, you must be specific. Throwing a ball in any direction and hoping that it will somehow make it in will never produce the results you want.

The other interesting point about the answer 'to be happy' is that you are pushing happiness beyond your reach. To be happy means that you have not achieved this yet, otherwise why are you trying to get something you already have? So, what are you missing which will make you happy; a car perhaps? Or that perfect job, or perfect partner? Yes, you would say, I'll be happy once I have…. so on and so forth. The issue with this is the fact that goals are not unmoving objects, they are heights which are constantly getting higher and higher. When you get that new job, you want to keep moving up, you want the next job. Goals are evolving with you as go through life achieving them.

What does this mean for your happiness? It is constantly being pushed further and further out of your reach.

Here is a little secret, look at that formula again. Quality + Quantity + Mental Attitude. The secret to achieving your goals or receiving higher compensation is getting yourself into a positive frame of mind before you start. There is a very popular class at Harvard University, which studies this exact concept. This class is called Positive Psychology. In fact, they have already conducted many tests on the influence of your mental attitude in regards to producing better outcomes. The results from these tests have shown that when you are positive, your energy levels rise, your creativity rises, your efficiency rises; all business outcomes improve. You are 37% better at sales! That is a pretty high percentage for something as simple as a Positive Mental Attitude.

Saying that what you want out of life is to be happy is the same thing as saying that what you want out of life is to survive. But we don't need to spend time on that anymore, how else are you going to use your time? This is the million-dollar question. This is why so many people feel unfulfilled; they believe satisfaction can come from the TV or perhaps a materialistic object. But these satisfactions are only temporary; they do not fill us up. True satisfaction comes from setting an inspiring goal, and working towards it. Happiness lies in aspiring, not acquiring.

We instantly feel better when we make a decision, but indecision can be a pernicious state of mind. Indecision is the reason why so many people procrastinate; in fact they are the same thing. So how do you set a major goal for your life, how do you decide what you want out of life?

This is one of most beneficial things you will get out of this principle of *Going the Extra Mile*. By applying this to your life in every possible way you can, you will receive one of the greatest compensations you can get; the compensation of uncovering your major purpose in life. It will help you to make the decision of what you really want to do. It helps you to select a major goal, and gives you the courage to go after it.

By now I am sure you understand what it is to Go the Extra Mile, but just in case, it is simply doing more than you are being compensated for. If you Go the Extra Mile, you are applying the formula of Q+Q+MA. This means that it will be impossible for you not to be compensated for any extra work that you do. Make it your business to provide as much Quality service to as many people (Quantity) as you can, with a Positive Mental Attitude. This formula is unbeatable and unstoppable, and the best part is: you do not have to ask anyone's permission to do it.

No one can stop you from applying this in your life, yet do not be too surprised if other people around you seem to be agitated at first by what you are doing. This is simply because no one likes to be shown up, because most people do not go the first mile, let alone the second. Like I said, most of us are bored, and some people like to sit on the sidelines of life and watch. If they see you passing by and it looks like you are going somewhere and they are not, they may stick their foot out to watch you fall, merely for their entertainment.

But do not let this bother you! Many great men and women of achievement have had to endure much criticism from others before their day of recognition came. Look at the Wright Brothers; after they had perfected a machine, which could fly, they called up all the local newspapers to come down and take a look. No one showed up. No one believed they could do it, but that did not mean it could not be done.

Elyse Hargreaves | Bio

Elyse Hargreaves first came across Napoleon Hill when she was 22 years old and from then on Napoleon has been her closest friend. Since a very young age Elyse has been very interested in the human mind, specifically what it was potentially capable of doing. The answer to her question was in Napoleon Hill's *Science of Success*, and this philosophy has added more meaning to her life than she could ever describe. After years of study, she has finally found her own Definite Major Purpose, and is currently engaged in studying her main field of interest, Philosophy of Science. This passion for science has guided her throughout her life, and my perhaps be attributed to her father; a mechanical engineer with a very strong attitude of critical analysis. Growing up, Elyse was always given the freedom to think for herself and find the answers on her own. This led her to studying science outside of school on her own terms, and throughout the years this has given her an unlimited source of enlightenment.

Elyse can be reached at elysehargreaves@gmail.com or on Twitter @ElyseHargreaves

CHAPTER 4

One Tiny Little Heart

By Michelle Casey

In 1983, at the tender age of 19, I took a leap of faith. I parked my idea of becoming an English History Teacher and ventured across the Atlantic Ocean to America. I left all I knew in my hometown of Nottingham, England to try my luck at living the "American Dream."

Upon arrival, I was dazzled by what I saw. I almost instantly fell in love with the sandy beaches and blue waters of the coastal shores of South Carolina. It's been almost 35 years since I made that first leap and I've not even once regretted it.

My first job in America was working in a beachside arcade as a monitor, issuing game coins to eager children. I'd landed the job because of an opening in my cousin's family business and felt blessed to have the entry level position.

After a time, other opportunities emerged and I began working in service and hospitality. This went on for a few years, until I found myself working breakfast shifts at a family owned waffle house. The 5am shift was not my first choice, but I was grateful to have a job. Besides, I was happy to be home early in the day. I enjoyed evenings with my family, as I was at that time married with a child.

The restaurant certainly didn't offer glamorous work. It most definitely was not an inspirational environment, promoting success and thought leadership. It was a place where most opted to endure the day rather than find ways to enjoy it. Many would have cringed at the idea of working there. Daily bickering between staff members regarding work responsibilities, as well as unkind remarks from complaining customers, made it quite dismal at times.

Despite that, I decided to do whatever I could to make it a better place to work. I thought that an ever-present cheerful smile would be a good place to start. I hoped that my eagerness would prove contagious, but alas, it did not. Instead, it baffled my co-workers when I would cheerfully volunteer to do the nastiest chores, especially when most staff members would do their utmost to avoid them. These chores included cleaning smelly bathrooms and draining slimy grease traps in the kitchen as well as mopping floors.

It was mind boggling to my co-workers that I could be so willing to take on anything. I seemed almost weird to them. They frequently asked me why I was so happy, as if I was keeping a secret from them. I would answer, "Why make things more miserable?"

One day, I was serving coffee to a customer who complimented my smile. He was a kind man, in his forties, who mentioned that he owned a beauty school. I soon learned that he had been monitoring my service. He remarked on my friendly disposition and said I would do well in the salon business. We struck up a conversation and I shared my story of how I had applied twice to Beauty School but was rejected because I didn't have an American High School Diploma. He said that if I was serious about applying, he knew a way to make it work. He extended an invitation for me to go to the school, and take a simple aptitude test. If I passed the test, I would be eligible to enroll in the program and start with the next class. After work, that same day, I went to the school and took the test.

My first day of school was just 2 weeks later. I fully recognized the opportunity before me and I was very excited. Beauty school was a wonderful place to be after being released from the breakfast diner. I loved the clean smells of shampoo and the sound of the blow dryers. I felt good dressed up wearing a spotless white lab jacket and experiencing the feel of a modern salon. I was ecstatic to learn new and creative things every day. I loved being in the classroom. I was hungry to learn everything I could and I aimed to be the best in every way. I was so eager that it appeared to annoy some of the other students who were less enthusiastic. It seemed that I asked too many questions in the classroom. Classmates often complained that I took my lessons too seriously causing extended class time. They teased me and I was tagged "Miss-By-The-Book" because I followed school protocols religiously.

Fortunately for me, not everyone felt that way about me. There was another like-minded student with whom I connected. We encouraged each other, and inadvertently formed a mastermind alliance. We worked side by side whenever possible and we were quickly recognized as a team.

The bonds of friendship were formed and our eyes were fixed on our plans for success. As young women, neither of us had yet heard of Napoleon Hill. Without really being aware of it, we had stumbled on several of his principles of achievement. As I reflect back now, I realize that the following principles were a part of our daily culture:

1. **Definite Major Purpose**
2. **Mastermind Alliance**
3. **Applied Faith**
4. **Going the Extra Mile**
5. **Positive Mental Attitude**
6. **Controlled Attention**
7. **Personal Initiative.**
8. **Team Work**

These principles were applied daily, but the one most openly recognized by others would have been *Going the Extra Mile*!

Opportunities often presented themselves when we were in school, and we were quick to act. One particular opportunity was offered to us exclusively. We were selected to travel to Atlanta, Georgia for an all expense paid learning opportunity, at a Skin Care Institute. The owner of our school said we were chosen because he felt that we were serious students who would not squander his investment. He knew we would willingly share our new information with other classmates upon our return. He squelched any jealousy amongst our peers by simply stating the same opportunity would be available for anyone willing to do the extra credit work we had done.

Extra Credits were earned by turning in assignments in a timely fashion, either on or before deadlines. Giving up weekends or optional holidays in exchange for the chance to graduate early was also an available choice. Ultimately, graduation came for me in a little more than nine months, instead of the usual allowance of twelve months. Ironically, going the extra mile actually shortened the distance!

Napoleon Hill teaches the following formula on "*Going the Extra Mile*":

Going the Extra Mile means rendering more service than is expected, with a positive mental attitude. *Going the Extra Mile* is demonstrated by the QQMA Formula:

Quality of service + Quantity of service + Mental Attitude = Compensation you get for your services.

The QQMA formula determines the space you occupy in your chosen calling. Benefits of following the QQMA formula:

1. Brings you to the attention of those who can provide you with opportunities.
2. Supports you in the law of increasing returns.
3. Makes you indispensable in your chosen calling and therefore able to write your own ticket.
4. Helps you excel in your line of work.
5. Increases respect from others.
6. Helps you develop a keen, alert imagination.
7. Inspires you to move on your own personal initiative.
8. Helps you to master procrastination.
9. Influences others to respect your integrity and inspires them to go out of their way to cooperate with you.
10. Creates favorable breaks.

The principles of *Going the Extra Mile* migrated from beauty school to my new work environment.

It was very early in my career, when I came upon a young bride-to-be needing a pedicure. Her wedding date was fast approaching and I was the assigned service provider. I was still a rookie and known as the" new- girl" in an established full service salon. I was both nervous and eager as I'd just launched into my new career in the salon industry.

After completing the service, I was both relieved and delighted that the young bride loved her freshly painted toes. She showed them off to her Aunt, who had treated her to the pedicure, and had stopped by the salon to pay.

Miss Brenda (the Aunt) suggested that a little white heart would be the perfect finishing touch on the newly painted, valentine- red toes. I flushed at the thought of performing the task, as I was so inexperienced in nail art. I was short on time, and even weaker in confidence. I pushed back my nervousness, and agreed enthusiastically, despite my concerns. I felt pressured because her disappointment loomed over me, and could drop at any moment if I failed. If I were to accidentally smudge the work, my creditability as a skilled professional would be lost. The young bride would have to endure the lengthy correction process of removing everything, and starting over with no guarantee of a perfect end result. I buckled down, smiled, and then said "I will be glad to add that special touch for you Miss Brenda." To my delight (and theirs) - it was a perfect tiny white heart. Phew!

While the nails were drying, I cleared it with my boss, suggesting that the tiny white heart would be my gift to them as a way of wishing them well for the upcoming nuptials. Miss Brenda and her niece seemed very touched. I had no idea that it meant so much to Miss Brenda.

As it turned out, that tiny little heart was an even bigger success for me than I could have ever imagined. Several years later, Miss Brenda walked into a different salon where I was working. She recognized me instantly and requested my services. She told me how much that tiny heart had meant and that she had never forgotten it. It was an instant connection and soon she became a regular client of mine.

We formed a very special relationship. I learned that Miss Brenda had been in the salon industry for over 30 years. She had been visiting with her niece at the former salon but found she did not enjoy the environment there. She recognized my inexperience and had picked up on my dilemma the day I painted that one, tiny, heart. She noted my eagerness to please and was very impressed with my attitude.

Over time, Miss Brenda became a mentor to me. She encouraged me to open my own salon. I eventually found a location but knew that I was not prepared financially. Without me knowing, Miss Brenda called her banker and asked him to call me. She told the banker to find out what I needed and instructed him to draw up paperwork for a bank loan. Ultimately, her intent was to co-sign and guarantee the loan. I was flabbergasted when I got the call from the banker. I thought I had won the lottery!

I contacted the owner of my former beauty school and consulted with him. He was delighted to hear about my success and my opportunity. He helped me design my salon and connected me to a contractor. I owned the salon for 10 years and paid back the loan within 3 years. I will be eternally grateful to the faith and kindness bestowed upon me. I went the extra- mile with one tiny little heart. Miss Brenda's heart was bigger than I could have ever imagined.

The story you have read here is only the beginning of the many blessings that I have received as a result of always being willing to go the extra mile.

I have been in the industry for over 28 years now and have enjoyed great success. I continue to practice Napoleon Hill's principles of achievement daily. They are a clear guide and plan for certain success. Going the extra mile is simply a positive mental attitude, in action.

It is now a habit that requires no thought. I find myself instinctively gravitating toward any way to manifest extra effort in both work and personal relationships. In essence, it has become effortless. However, I must add a cautionary note to the givers in this world:

Givers will create takers, so it is important that you do not become a slave to any particular individual who is consuming your efforts for their own personal gain. Be a wise and mindful giver by carefully choosing whom you will give time and effort to endlessly. Going the extra mile is a good thing in almost any situation, even if the recipient of your good deed appears to be ungrateful. If it goes undetected, don't be discouraged. Keep your mind sharp to obvious predators and your heart always open to possibility.

Going the extra mile is often a wonderful experience, especially when it is for the greater good, and is inspired from a heart full of love. Taking a first step from the heart, gives you the heart to go the extra mile---- no matter how tiny, that one little heart, is. Don't be afraid to take the tiny first step!

Michelle Casey | Bio

Michelle was born and raised in England and immigrated to America in 1983. She became a proud American citizen, after being awarded citizenship in 1997.

Her career started in the salon industry as a young hairstylist, advancing as a salon owner and National Educator for John Paul Mitchell Systems. Michelle was also fortunate enough to be introduced to N.A.M.I (National Alliance for Mental Illness), leading her to volunteer in their family support program and serve on the Board.

Michelle is also a Certified Professional Life Coach offering workshops and seminars in communications and personal development. In 2015, she also became a Certified Leader for the Napoleon Hill Foundation.

She enjoys being an active member in the National Speakers Association. Michelle is a member of Toastmasters International and serves as President in her local area.

Public speaking and education have become her passion. This led to the development of HairCology™, which establishes communication formats for salon industry professionals and their clients. Michelle specializes in teaching techniques focused on removing communication blocks and emotional tangles in the salon chair.

You can reach Michelle directly through either of the following:

Book details on Your Hairy Godmother- Hair Trauma Preventionist go to: www.YourHairyGodmother.com and www.HairCology101.com

CHAPTER 5

Going the Extra Myles

By Jerrilynn Rebeyka.

The Kind of Guy You Want to Marry

ASK ANNIE:

My dad wants me to finish college before I tie the knot. But I've met a worldly man named Myles and he's absolutely DREAMY! He has a fresh face, a clean attitude and he is warm and friendly. Myles is so profound – he sees everything with greater meaning and he knows where he is going. He's always there; so close to me. But I never tire of him. He's not clingy and annoying like the last guy. He's the kind of guy who always throws his heart into everything he does! Everyone we associate with welcomes him with open arms. In fact, he's become quite crucial to my life and countless others. He really shines when we are alone but when there's a crowd - that's when the sparks fly! I love him so much and I know together we can make all our dreams come true. I can't let him slip away just because my parents believe the timing isn't right for their daughter. But they are paying my tuition bills. Do you think I should stop seeing him? – ATTEMPTING TO CUT THE UMBILICAL CORD

DEAR CUT THE CORD:

Cut the Cord! This man sounds like a life partner and every girl's dream. If you don't marry him, I will! Your parents will be accepting of him when they meet. Sounds like he acts with definiteness of purpose. The superior way he treats you and the assistance he provides to your circle of contacts is outstanding. Most people are not willing to put themselves out there unless they are being adequately compensated. He sets himself apart as indispensable. But before you make any long-term plans, hang out with him until college is done to ensure these are engrained behaviours. Observing this type of solidity in his actions produces reliability and predictability in the relationship; two things you will be very grateful for in years to come. Best of luck! And send me a wedding photo!

Ask Annie has enough information from her brief interaction with the column reader to determine that CUT THE CORD girl has already incorporated Myles permanently into her life. One might say that Myles has become her habit (albeit a good one!)

Myles is a familiar and fascinating fellow. Most people get a smile on their face when you mention his name. My kids happen to know Myles and describe him as working hard to accomplish something and willing to run the whole race. A friend likened Myles to the concept of Paying It Forward and a business associate to the idea of goodwill. These statements might sum him up but this generic labeling is stereotypical if we prejudge him without an in-depth understanding of his character traits. A long lasting and fruitful relationship will only come from fully embracing his entire demeanor on a continual basis.

Students of the philosophy behind "*Think and Grow Rich*" get the gratifying experience of dissecting the aspects of Napoleon Hills' description of "Myles" and his many great features! He is not complicated; just sophisticated. Many people believe they are using this principle – correctly termed *GOING THE EXTRA MILE* - but they are simply referring to themselves conquering life's challenges. As tough as some of those obstacles can be, this use of the term does not encapsulate the spirit of rendering extra service over and above what is expected while maintaining a positive attitude and always striving for ultimate achievement. Just as it is recommended you accept the whole person when entering into marriage, and not just the parts you currently like or are familiar with, you need to embrace all aspects of this principle as Hill describes it. With this caveat, I wish to proceed with a focus on the Service piece knowing this will eventually lead us towards a commitment to the whole principle. Let us put a ring on one finger of the many pronged principle of *GOING THE EXTRA MILE*: Making quality and quantity of service part of daily life!

You may ask:

1. How do you know if you have locked arms with Myles? i.e. If you have made a commitment to providing the type of service that equates to GOING THE EXTRA MILE?
2. How much time should you spend with Myles? i.e. How often should you provide this type of service to get desired results?

Myles is the kind of guy that likes to do high performance workouts! *GOING THE EXTRA MILE* is the principle of activity. Taking action, gets results and

> *"the law of compensation which is called into action by your activities will always do something for you."*
>
> — Napoleon Hill.

The best modus operandi is at the HIGH end of the scale. Here, height is a subjective measure but essentially means the best you have to offer. Since compensation follows service, you will not be able to tell ahead of time if you have administered enough and may require additional attempts and added gumption. Superior service drives favorable compensation. Sometimes compensation comes in an unexpected form (maybe not money but peace of mind, harmonious relations, skill development...) or in an unexpected timeframe. But asking, "Have I done enough?" to be compensated means you are not operating in the right spirit. None of Dr. Hill's principles focus on minimums. *GOING THE EXTRA MILE* is one of the fundamentals of the philosophy and means going beyond what is expected. Do not expect to ever rise above mediocrity without it. Service always comes back greatly multiplied as per the Law of Increasing Returns. *GOING THE EXTRA MILE* pays off in proportion to the intensity with which you apply it. Therefore, do it in the proportion to the kind of success you are looking for. The bottom line is stop dawdling along in life and get busy. Know that the more aligned your activities are with your Definite Major Purpose, the more of your desired success you will experience.

Myles's twin brother, Percy (Personal Initiative) is needed to GO THE EXTRA MILE as well as things like PMA and determination, persistence through Self Discipline, and a Pleasing Personality. Even Myles cannot go it alone; we all need family and friends! Hill's principles always overlap with one another and continually stress the importance of embracing the whole philosophy for utmost success.

Myles is the kind of guy who is generous and altruistic. There is a natural law at work when you decide to operate like Myles. Basically, you reap what you sow according to the Law of Compensation. If you give out positive energy or negativity in thoughts and deeds, you will receive back the same. You do not necessarily have to be operating without the expectation of a reward. However, whether you are or not, it is inevitable that you will be compensated beyond what you have exerted. Ultimately, you should be operating in a freehearted mode without regard for perceived limits of any potential immediate compensation.

Myles is a "quality" kind of guy. How you do anything is how you do everything. This means that everything you say or do ultimately forms the life you experience. No matter if you are scrubbing floors or performing surgery, speaking to your kids at the supper table or delivering a formal speech to the nation – do it with pride and integrity, meaning and substance. There is value in adding some *GOING THE EXTRA MILE* spice. The majority of people will not pay attention to how they do anything. Therefore, by the Law of Contrast, you can stand out to those who may hold opportunity for you in their hands. You can start right now with every serviceable activity to do it greater than you are now being paid. You do not have to ask anyone's permission because no one will mind. "How you do anything" is about forming good habits and patterns. Introducing Myles' good buddy: Cosmos! Where there is order, such as we have in nature and space, there is predictable action and reaction which Hill termed Cosmic Habitforce:

> *"You are where you are and what you are*
> *because of your Established Habits of*
> *Thoughts and Deeds."*
>
> — Napoleon Hill

So, practice *GOING THE EXTRA MILE* in your daily life. When it becomes subconscious and simply part of who you are, Cosmic Habitforce has taken over. Myles is a predictable kind of guy. To mimic

33

what works for him, just do the highest quality and quantity of work far beyond what is expected. Do it consciously until it becomes engrained in your state of being.

There are many examples of outstanding people who have engrained the concept of *GOING THE EXTRA MILE* throughout history. First to mind is Napoleon Hill, who worked diligently and unwaveringly; essentially uncompensated for twenty years to develop this philosophy. Another lifelong mile maker is Oprah Winfrey. An extraordinary role model, Oprah oozes giving with no expectation of receipt. Her admirable and flawless example of *GOING THE EXTRA MILE* has left her highly compensated financially with the Law of Increasing Returns kicking in a million-fold. It is in direct proportion to the volumes of service and love she has given this world far beyond any benefits received at the time giving it. She did not always have a TV show or celebrity status allowing her to give on a grand scale. But her big heart aching to help the world heal on so many levels is always working towards that end. And now the blessings she has received back in her life from helping others far exceeds the financial compensation.

GOING THE EXTRA MILE is best observed in nature. Anytime you align with nature's laws you will be in the flow of the universal energy or Infinite Intelligence where you are guaranteed to succeed. My middle child has continually pleaded with me in subtle ways to appreciate nature and its quiet beauty. One instance of my awakening occurred this past summer. With this chapter idea not yet forthcoming, I was reminded of Hill's discussion of the orderliness of the universe; predictable and reliable in all of its operations. Our family of five, normally stirring up chaos and "un-orderliness", each vying for the microphone, experienced an awesome example of how nature goes the extra mile. My husband, Mike, and I, recently having had our own mortality take a hard stare back at us over the last year, intended to spend the summer looking for more tranquility and family time. We were staying at my husband's childhood home. Everyone was tired and emotional after a long week. My mother-in-law had taken a hard fall leading to cardiac arrest and was now waiting for hip surgery. Since things appeared to be progressing towards recovery, we decided to travel back to our house. An early morning meant an early bedtime; not an easy feat on summer holidays but also with out of the ordinary sleeping arrangements and two giggling sisters. In preparation for a quick morning get away, I asked Mike to take out the garbage before retiring for the night. There was no way I was going around the dark side of the house in the quiet shadows of this little town. I did not feel like ending up in a staring contest with a skunk or feeling the chill of the coyotes howling during the short walk to the bins. On returning to the house, he had the look of a kid on Christmas morning and he said, "Jerri, we have to take the kids for a drive. The northern lights are so spectacular you will not believe it." I was about to say no because they had just quieted, when I realized I was not winning that argument. So, we loaded the kids up in their pyjamas in the truck. It was already a little cool and dewy which added to the ambiance of the excursion. I felt like Laura Ingalls' "Ma" loading the kids up for a wagon trip through the prairie! We headed out of town and turned down a dark country road, the only thing cutting the blackness was our headlights and a yard light so far off in the distance it looked like a low hanging star itself. Topping the scene was a mesmerizing array of vibrant sprays of light up above. Coinciding with a meteor shower that night, shooting stars were blasting by faster than wishes could be made. Magnificent and eerie, we stood in awe and felt our insignificance under the massive blanket of sparkling green haze that capped us like a dome. The temptation to take pictures was powerless against the etching of the dancing lights in our memories. I thought about nature's abundance in its production of beauty. The beholder reaps the benefits of this magnificent harvest in the joy of the experience. However, as with the rendering of service unwillingly or resentfully, with the wrong mindset, you risk getting nothing back. I almost missed out by staying in the truck with my oldest daughter, being more concerned about comfort – getting bit by mosquitos, being cold, and fearing wild animals!

Nothing shows the fine details of nature's magnificent spectacles better than the photography of Louie Schwartzberg. Mr. Schwartzberg has combined the principle AND its best case in point by *GOING THE EXTRA MILE* with nature at the core of much of his moving art. He is a filmmaker with a view to capturing time lapsed imagery and says this about his purpose;

> *"If I can move enough people on an*
> *emotional level, I hope we can achieve the*
> *shift in consciousness we need to sustain*
> *and celebrate life."*

— https://movingart.com/louie-schwartzberg/

He has been shooting film continuously for over three decades. One of the results of his tireless, and then uncompensated, efforts has been a gift to the world in terms of awareness. In spending copious amounts of time, he delicately captured the intricate scheme nature has for pollination of flowers; leaving the viewer feeling like Alice down the rabbit hole marveling at a world of which we are so unaware.

The contributions of these people and countless others that have embraced this principle throughout time are immeasurable. None of them used *GOING THE EXTRA MILE* exclusively (bringing into play such principles as Definite Major Purpose, Controlled Attention, and Self Discipline to attain a goal), but they definitely modeled themselves after nature with respect to *GOING THE EXTRA MILE*. How do the majority of people, who believe they use the principle, differ in their behavior from those I mentioned? Habit.

I have used this principle successfully in my own life multiple times but I have also failed to use it. Notice I did not say the principle failed. It is rock solid and works faithfully when properly implemented. As a student of the philosophy and a business owner in a company that strongly recommends thorough knowledge and utilization of the Hill's Success Principles, I realized I have NOT implemented it the way nature or Dr. Hill intended. I have done little spurts. For instance, after my first baby was born, myself and a co-worker realized that, in comparison to standards and other companies, our supplemental maternity leave benefits were out of line. We fought tirelessly for several years knowing that we ourselves would likely never see any of the substantial financial benefit from doing so. However, we knew that others before us had fought for the benefits we enjoyed as employees. We achieved our goal and the compensation was the satisfaction of making things right. Another situation was several years ago when we lived in a neighboring town. My husband and I were very involved in the community. It was where we purchased our first home and planned to raise our family. I voluntarily started a community association with an initiative to build a children's spray park. Although we moved and it may never come to fruition, we did raise tens of thousands of dollars. Success did not come in the format I was expecting but I was more than compensated in the benefits that I received in giving of myself. I improved my professional skills, formed relationships with people I may not otherwise have met, and, unbeknownst to me at the time, I implemented many of Dr. Hill's other principles such as Definiteness of Purpose and Self-Discipline. Not to mention my kids thought that I was the boss of the town! A third example was my second pregnancy, which ended in a tumultuous tragedy. After weeks of odd discharges and sickening worry (which probably did not help) constant running to the doctor for careful monitoring, ultrasounds, and tests, we finally got some breathing space when things appeared to have settled down. Naively I thought that I was out of the woods reaching the second trimester. Then suddenly one night around 19 weeks, my temperature spiked. We rushed to the hospital where my husband watched in horror as our little girl was born too early and I became septic. Reaching out through my heartache, I attempted to start a support group. *GOING THE EXTRA MILE* for other women in similar circumstances, I received the most amazing friendships with two of the strongest women I know.

But *GOING THE EXTRA MILE* cannot be sporadic. Nothing has taught us that lesson better than our network marketing business. In the beginning, it was difficult to see success for all the obstacles. We were doing road trips, business meetings, and sampling potential customers at our own expense. We were helping people get their businesses started where the time we invested was not financially compensated. Before we reached the first leadership level, we were seeing a disillusioned world where people were mistrusting our motives based on false beliefs about the industry we operate in. But thanks to many people who have GONE THE EXTRA MILE before us, such as Eric Worre (who has dispelled the myths and changed the face of network marketing) and all predecessor distributors with huge success who approached people in an ethical manner with a viable business plan, network marketing is fast being recognized as one of the most secure, low cost, attractive business models that exist today. It is not always easy to render service especially where people are skeptical and mistrusting of your motives. They can only be convinced by continually providing spectacular service in an exuberant manner. We do not get paid until we first work hard at becoming a trusted example to follow.

Learning this philosophy is in itself *GOING THE EXTRA MILE*. Whether it is "Percy" initiated or some mandatory training requirement, the activities of exploring the principles and implementing them effectively into your daily life are first done without compensation. Every ounce of study and practice will improve your ability to provide both a high quality and quantity of service. Compensation will be especially bountiful should you formally study the philosophy through the Napoleon Hill Foundation allowing you to add this highly prestigious certification to your bio or resume. Even this publication and the other books in this series were created by *GOING THE EXTRA MILE*. The authors write and pay for publishing with the purpose of promoting the Napoleon Hill Foundation philosophy. Their intent is to help others benefit from its teachings at least as much as they have.

I believe I have GONE THE EXTRA MILE in many instances but more is necessary; my greatest compensation is forthcoming. I am still a student of this philosophy and a baby eagle taking flight in the MLM business. Rendering this level of service must be inherent in everything I do and say and in every aspect of my being. Only then can I expect the magnitude of success I am looking for in this life. You can see by the examples of grandeur in nature and the extraordinary people I highlighted, that making a habit out of *GOING THE EXTRA MILE* is imperative for monumental success. If you are not doing it 100% of the time, you run the risk of missing an opportunity that could be key:

"A single simple incident as the drama of your life unfolds may prove to be a pivotal point around which your future destiny will revolve. That is why we should continually stress the advisability of practicing the principle not just on occasion. By continually availing yourself of this privilege you are accumulating a credit balance in the eternal ledger which, when you need it most will pay you a dividend in one form or another."

— Napoleon Hill

We have the ability to choose to harmonize with these laws of life. It is "through the exercise of this divine gift man has a voluntary avenue of approach to Infinite Intelligence. This means that he can place the forces of the entire universe behind his plans and purposes." – Napoleon Hill

So, way to go CUT THE CORD girl! Marry that Myles and set the example. Just Ask Annie and ask Dr. Hill if *GOING THE EXTRA MILE* is a habit worth espousing for life!

Jerrilynn Rebeyka | Bio

Jerrilynn Rebeyka is an independent distributor for ORGANO™ (OG) - a global network marketing company that carries a variety of premium everyday healthier living products including coffee, tea and protein shakes. She has been married to her husband and business partner Mike for twenty years and they have three remarkable children.

Jerrilynn's background is in Accounting with a CMA-CPA designation and a Bachelor of Commerce degree. She has 25 years of experience in telecommunications. An avid volunteer, she founded a Community Association in her former town. Throughout health challenges, she has become a Wellness Champion (via Pam Bartha) and achieved her Reiki Level I.

Jerrilynn desires to revamp fundraising and to nurture the traditional family dynamic with a focus on youth. These goals will be fueled by her addiction to personal development, which flourished during leadership training at both OG University and through the Napoleon Hill Foundation. In reaching her goals, she will assist others to change their mindset towards achievement of their greatest purpose.

She is an Amazon bestselling co-author of *Beyond "What If?"*, and intends to pursue more writing. A longstanding proponent that All is Well and that we should all live from an intention to Give Into Life, Jerrilynn can be contacted at:

beyondcoffeerow@sasktel.net

beyondcoffeerow.myorganogold.com

CHAPTER 6

An Appointment With Our True Greatness

By Francisco Mendoza

Science and Philosophy of Yesterday and Today

The great philosophers, as well as the most innovative scientists, influential writers, and all the characters that have played a role in universal transcendentalism. They created deep footprints in human evolution by transforming, in one way or another, different cultures, their way of living and the way we look at things in time and distance. They have given us tools to visualize with greater clarity and accuracy, from the real to the unimaginable. And, even though the process would bring as a positive consequence readiness to wholly identify the adaptation to the deserved individual development; the controversy of the emotional and the intellectual impedes identification of the best interpretations about learning.

"I've never let schooling interfere with my education", said the father of American literature Mark Twain (1835-1910), who with great wisdom gives a warning with that keen message. This phrase will be the backbone that will help us understand what for many personal growth perspectives is insufficient to improve ourselves as people and adequately prepare for desired success. Without under-appreciating the contributions of the great philosopher, mathematician, and scientist, Rene Descartes (1596-1650), father of modern philosophy and creator of rationalist philosophy, who said: (Cogito Ergo Sum) "I think, therefore I am", a phrase that although small in size, is large because of the polemical impact it had and still has in many people who try to reach goals. In the majority of cases those dreams do not become luminous stars, perhaps because with this phrase he was not referring to the thought that generates those emotions, but thought as an intellectual factor.

It is because in his opus "The Six Metaphysical Meditations" he gives all credit to intellect for the accomplishments achieved by people, canceling the value of emotions in its entirety, which is known as the "Descartes' dualism". This concept, to me, is an incorrect thesis that became very influential, even in the heart of Harvard University, where even with its prestige many years ago it was taboo to discuss the influence of the emotions on the biological part of the human being.

To this belief of Descartes we have been paying homage and have believed that without a proper academic preparation it's difficult or impossible to reach success, so therefore if we are forced to perform a job that is not of our liking nor compensates us as we would want or deserve, we always have the comfortable argument: (I work here because I didn't go to college), which is the poorest and sorriest excuse with which we have created our "beautiful" comfort zone, but is far from comfortable.

In contrast with the Six Metaphysical Meditations, such situations would be saved by Blaise Pascal (1623-1662), child prodigy, Christian philosopher, physics mathematician, writer, inventor, who said: "The heart has its reasons of which reason knows nothing". Pascal was younger than Descartes, which is maybe why humanity gave more credibility to the Six Metaphysical Meditation legacy with which we have been dealing with today.

Like Pascal, other philosophers, investigators, and scientists have presented impeccable and accurate precepts, but Descartes's print is still fresh and in force.

Today we all have a moral obligation to ourselves since we must discover our best self. Even if it's difficult to accept, today's proposal is not to learn something new, but to unlearn all those habits that can cause us so much harm.

During a vacation to New York, with my children Khristine and Francisco III and my wife, we visited the Metropolitan Museum of Art, where we enjoyed many marvels, including some perfect statues that caught our eye. On this occasion, my friend and colleague Tom Cunningham invited me to participate in this book project, just as he did with other colleagues from different parts of the world, who are also Napoleon Hill Foundation instructors. While I was observing the sculptures with great admiration, Michelangelo's (1475-1574) "David" came into my mind, who after three years of visualization and work, produced from a big bucket of marble, what many consider his greatest masterpiece. The greatest sculptor of all times when asked about the level of perfection said; "David was in that block, I merely chipped off what was unnecessary".

To keep exploring parts unknown until I am sure that we can find some light, and to put the Six Metaphysical Meditations in relieve once more, I will allow myself to quote the director of the Milan Brain Institute, who said in a conference; "Genius is born and idiocy is accomplished", when a member of the audience asked, "And what's in between?" he responded, "The system in which we are educated". This is proof that the environmental contamination, familiar or social, people – sometimes beloved to us- in our surroundings have infected us negatively, saturating us with disqualifying labels, that we have ended up accepting verbatim as the only reality, which is why many of our failures are because of such imposed limitations to the aforementioned genius.

Before he died, Steve Jobs (1955-2011), the American Co-Founder of Apple Computers was asked the reason for his success, and he responded that it was his passion for his projects. That was the only reason he survived so many pitfalls and adversities, because if he had not been like that, he would have given up and never seen his accomplishments.

Jobs' answer tells us that the main element for success in any project is the power of emotions, and here is where Pascal gives his checkmate to the Six Metaphysical Meditations, because what the heart desires, the brain makes possible. In no university does the subject of passion or enthusiasm exist yet. These two emotions give life to the creative vision, a key element for success.

The Spanish writer Noel Claraso I. Serrat (1905-1985) said: "Throw your heart over first and your horse will jump the obstacle. Many faint before the obstacle. They failed to throw their heart into it first." Remember that to reach true success in any purpose, we must fall in love with what we embark upon because a person will do for love that which he or she would never do for money. On one occasion a reporter visited Mother Theresa of Calcutta and looking at her kiss the face of a sick man in deplorable conditions, commented: "I wouldn't do that for a million euros", to which she responded, "Me neither."

Enthusiasm and Passion are essential for success to be decisive, since Passion is the mother of Creative Vision. Since we have been talking about great people, we must mention the authority in neuroscience of his time, Don Santiago Ramon y Cajal (1852-1934), scientist and doctor specializing in histology and pathological anatomy. He said; "Each human being can be, if he wants it, the sculptor of his own brain." Here is where we must take the initiative to understand and make changes that we need to conquer true success. Don Santiago had seen that when we feel excited and impassioned about a certain situation, then the Cajal's dendritic spines, which he discovered himself (hence carrying his name), proliferated and allowed greater access to neuroplasticity, that connection of neurons that make us more intelligent beings. Today, thanks to studies in the Salk Institute of La Joya in San Diego, California and the Karolinska Institute of Stockholm, Sweden, it has been proven through profound studies about the brain, that stem cells travel from the ventricles among other parts to the hippocampus, which is the center of memory and learning, and that also has the capacity to deactivate the cerebral amygdale when it has been activated through a false alarm; and after 21 days neurogenesis occurs, which means the creation of 500 to 1000 new neurons daily, this said in simple language we become more intelligent, and this could be proven with people up to 82 years old. Even though in Cajal's time there were no positron-emitting helmets, or functional magnetic resonance or neuro-imagery to witness such phenomenon, he correctly surmised that this way, which what it is fair to conclude, that if we are of a positive mental attitude, even facing pitfalls and adversity, such neurogenesis will form new neural circuits that will allow us to meet the best version of ourselves.

The brain can be trained to work in our favor and in the best way, but it requires true compromise, to make ourselves the promise to truly exercise our freedom to take correct decisions especially before pitfalls and adversity. Today, it is important to detract from a reference by the neurologist and American scientist, Benjamin Libet (1916-2007), pioneer in the field of conscience, whose studies doubted the freedom of human being, since we know that it is true that we are indeed free.

Libet's thesis is sustained in studies performed in 1979, where he used electroencephalographic equipment to demonstrate (supported by neurobiologists) that the brain makes the decision and then the person experiences the decision, associating the decision with its own freedom of doing. That was an indicator that was used to imply that the human being does not make decisions in a conscious way, but rather as a result of an already established determined neural circuit to which we respond automatically, even though in reality human beings have decided for ourselves to be free or not be free and that is the best evidence of our freedom.

Without a doubt, whenever we decide to leave our "comfort zone", we embark on that voyage towards an encounter with our best version, and we begin then to change our mental schemes, responding to other neural circuits in order to make more precise decisions in a conscious way, which means that without a doubt the time will come after 21 days in which we will act better in the face of adversities and we will become more capable of reaching what we resolve to do. This could be called Unconscious Efficiency, in other words we will end up doing automatically what is correct and effective without us noticing.

During the investigation performed by Dr. Napoleon Hill from 1906 to 1926, time in which he established the 16 laws of success, there was still no technology that could prove such profound changes in the brain, same which create moods. From there, said author explains to us in his book *"Think and Grow Rich"*, that people who followed the mentioned precepts verbatim, were able to conquer what they resolved to do. There is testimony from many millionaires that were inspired to reach great fortunes in *"Think and Grow Rich"*, same that inspired Dr. Hill to establish Law Number 17.

The wealth of any class comes from fervent desire and adding this to organized plans and ideas, it results in incredibly powerful elements that when they are mixed with precision, purpose, and persistence, they can transform into unimaginable accomplishments.

In my case, I was a candidate for failure, since I come from a humble family, for which it was almost impossible to contemplate success, since our culture, many times, does not allow us to visualize ourselves beyond what we are for the time. Therefore; being of humble parents and at times not having the means even for something to eat, was enough to not have the right to success; nevertheless understanding that it is impossible not to give proper credit to my family and friends who bet and believed on me and had priceless support gestures towards me and gave me always wise advise and inspirations, elements that played an essential role in my realization and in braking free of paradigms of the past, as possibly faults in personality or financial limitations which I was always willing to correct. Now I am conscious of the prosperous life I have always aspired to, in the same way resolving to forge my ever more promising future with absolute freedom.

Francisco Mendoza | Bio

Public Speaker and Instructor of the Napoleon Hill Foundation

Francisco Mendoza came to the United States when he was 19 years old, at the age of 27 he had owned a furniture factory in California, by 30 he owned a mortgage company. Today he is the owner and Designated Broker of Arizona Sonora Real Estate Group LLC, DBA At Home Real Estate AZ, and a Certified Real Estate Instructor in the State of Arizona. Real Estate Investor and Producer and co presenter of three radio programs "Quien es Quien en Bienes Raíces", an educational Real Estate Program that has been on the air for over seven years. Private Pilot licensed for 20 years. Director of Public Relations of the Hispanic Communities Council in USA and former Member of the Advisory Board of the Institute of Mexicans Abroad. Founder of the "Stop Fraud against Hispanics" Seminars. Author of "El Manual del Éxito en 21 Lecciones" (The success manual in 21 lessons). Napoleon Hill Foundation certified Instructor since 2008. Establishing the Success institute, (Instituto del Exito) in Arizona www.exitousa.com in 2009. Founding both the Latin-American Association of Real Estate Professionals in Phoenix Arizona and the Latin - American Chamber of Commerce in Phoenix AZ.

Francisco Mendoza

Author / /Instructor

Contact information:

Tel. 602-989-2929

Email broker@azmyhouse.com

Address: 3610 N. 44th Street Ste. 130

Phoenix, AZ 85018

Conferencista e Instructor de la Fundación Napoleón Hill

Francisco Mendoza llegó a los Estados Unidos a los 19 años de edad, a sus 27 años ya era dueño de una fabrica de muebles en California. Cumpliendo los 30 años de edad fue dueño de una compañía de prestamos hipotecarios, hoy por hoy es Dueño y Corredor de Bienes Raíces de Arizona Sonora Real Estate Group LLC DBA At Home Real Estate Arizona. Actualmente Instructor e Inversionista en Bienes Raíces en el estado de Arizona, además se ser Piloto Aviador por más de 20 años. Productor y co-conductor por más de siete años ininterrumpidos al aire en AM del Programa de radio "Quien es Quien en Bienes Raíces" con un programa educativo en Radio AM y dos programas en Radio FM. Director de Relaciones Públicas en EEUU del Consejo de Comunidades Hispanas después de haber sido Consejero del Instituto de Los Mexicanos en el Exterior. Coordinador de Foros Informativos de Migración y fundador de los seminarios "Alto al Fraude Contra el Hispano". Conferencista e Instructor Certificado de la Fundación Napoleón Hill. Author de "El Manual del EXITO" y Fundador del Instituto del Exito www.exitousa.com. Fundador de la Asociación Latinoamericana de Profesionistas en Bienes Raíces y la Cámara de Comercio Latinoamericana en Phoenix AZ.

Francisco Mendoza

Autor / Instructor

Contacto:

Tel. 602-989-2929

Correo Electrónico: broker@azmyhouse.com

Dirección: 3610 N. 44th Street Ste. 130

Phoenix, AZ 85018

CHAPTER 7

Secret Recipe To Guaranteed Success

By Mani Maran

Introduction:

In order to write a chapter for this book, I was thinking about the victories I had in my life. After doing some soul searching and reflection, one principle that stood out the most for me is *Going the Extra Mile*. If you are looking for the magic formula, shortcut, or guaranteed success, or want to do just one thing and be successful in your life, make a habit of going the extra mile. You have come to the right place and are reading the right book. If you burn this one idea into your heart and mind, you are going to reap rich rewards. I can tell you this with conviction; it has worked for me all the time.

How I came to the United States

I dreamt about getting a job in the United States when I was working in India in the IT field. On my first job, I was lucky to work with a great manager, Edwin. We always collaborated and exchanged ideas and implemented best solutions for our group. I worked very hard. I remember working many nights in succession to meet the project deadlines. Since I worked very hard, I always had a sound technical knowledge. The major barrier in getting a job in the US is not technical skills but the communication skills. Since I came from a village, though my English was not bad, I had issues communicating with professionals outside of India. So my linguistic skills acted as a roadblock to get a job in my dream country.

A work around to get hired in the United States is gaining work experience in another foreign county. I took my first opportunity to go oversees and went to Saudi Arabia. Most people passed up on their opportunity to go to Saudi Arabia because there was no entertainment there. I went on a one-year contract. I left my wife behind, who was pregnant with our first baby, to take on this opportunity, but promised to return soon after the baby was born.

The consulting company that hired me took my passport and gave me a letter. This letter was written in Arabic and mentioned the city I stayed in and the company I worked for. With this letter I was allowed to stay only in Riyadh. If I wanted to go to another city, I would need to get a different letter from my employer or the police would arrest me for an Illegal stay. Police roam around the city all the time and they speak very little English.

I lived in Saudi Arabia during the winter months; I had a hard time getting adjusted to the harsh dessert winter. I also stayed there during Ramadan months. During Ramadan, no one is allowed to eat from sunrise to sunset while in public. This rule is applicable to people from all religions. If a non-Muslim needs to eat during the day, they have to hide in a closet and eat food. This was very hard during working hours.

When most of the world has Saturday and Sunday off from work, Saudi had Thursdays and Fridays off.

I went the extra mile in Saudi Arabia with no family, no entertainment, and no life. I was able to do well. My manager, co-workers, and everyone around me liked my work. One of the best parts about living in Saudi Arabia was that I did not have to pay any income taxes. Unfortunately, I was paid based on my Nationality. Since I was from India I got paid a lot less than my western counterparts. But I was happy to learn the latest technologies and enjoy the benefit of making more money.

After I returned from Saudi, my chances of coming to US improved. I had gained experience with the latest technologies and improved my communication skills as well. These additional skills helped me get a job in the US in June, 1994.

How I tripled my Income

After I came to the US, I worked harder than I ever had. My first job was to train one developer as a database admin. In my free time in the evenings, I prepared myself to do more by learning some of the new features and functionalities of the complex database system.

I went to bookstores to read technology books. I subscribed to email lists, discussion groups, and technical journals to gather additional knowledge. I ate, lived and breathed the technical world.

I moved from Philadelphia to Dallas and back to Scranton, PA during my first two years in the US. I lived in Dallas during the summer and in Scranton during the winter, which is not a good choice. Temperatures get really high during the summers in Texas. During my stay in Dallas, I remember leaving an audiocassette in the car near the windshield and coming back to see the audiocassette melted. When I lived in Scranton, I experienced snow almost every day. I faced a six-foot blizzard during one winter day. I had seen extreme weather on both ends of the scale within one year. Then I moved to NJ and have been living here for the last 20 years.

During my work in India and Saudi Arabia, I used to read manuals from vendors. Manuals are good for reference, but are difficult to read. After coming to the US, I became fascinated with reading books written by experts in the field. I really got hooked on reading technical books. Books were fun to read and gave the perspective of the authors. Borders bookstore was my favorite place to buy and read books. I used to travel 20+ miles on weekends to go to the bookstore to get immersed in technical books.

One of my strengths is troubleshooting and solving technical problems and I used it as an opportunity to learn the complex software. I won't easily give up on any problem and go the extra mile solving problems. By continuing to gather additional information related to the problem, I gained expertize in the software field. With all these extra mile efforts, my income doubled within 3 and half years.

Doubling my income in less than 4 years was a major milestone for me and I did not stop my efforts there. I kept working harder and smarter. I became an expert with the Oracle database products and was hired by Oracle Corporation to work as their sub-contractor. I worked on projects for many fortune 500 companies while representing Oracle.

My manager was so impressed by my technical abilities that he wanted to hire me as a full-time employee. He started processing papers for my H1 B visa. My employer learned about this and countered Oracle's offer. They raised my salary even before my annual review was due and went the extra mile in taking care of my needs.

When I came to the US, my initial plan was to stay for 6 years – that was how long a professional could stay on a H1B visa then. I planned to go back to India to stay close to my parents once my visa expired. I did not pay attention to the green card processing that is needed for permanent residency in the US during my first five years. My employer reached out and asked me if I was interested in processing my green card in an expedited manner. I was not sure so I told them that I would give it a try. They substituted my case with someone similar to my case who had quit the company. This helped me stay in the US after the 6 years was over. It is very rare for a consulting to company to do that. Since I was one of their top consultants, I was lucky to be treated with this special benefit. I continued my journey of working hard and at the end of 7 years I had tripled my income and received my green card.

One idea that got burnt into my mind was; Do your duty and don't bother about the results. I think this was the essence of Karma. I did not work hard for the purpose of tripling my income or getting special treatment. I simply worked hard to become the best that I can be in my field. I was rewarded with more than I asked for. This is another example of the dividends of *going the extra mile.*

From non-runner to marathoner

A running coach spotted my second son from his high school as a good prospect for his cross-country team. Though reluctant at first, once he joined the team, he became motivated to be a good runner. He ran 30-40 miles a week to train for a 5K race. I was very impressed with his dedication and hard work and wanted to run myself. I started my first 5K race in the Fall of 2013 and managed to finish the race. Then I eyed a half marathon during the spring of 2014. I did my research and found Chi-running as a method that I wanted to follow. I prepared really well. I enrolled for the Chi-running classes and worked with Chi running coaches for private one-on-one training. I managed to complete my first Half-Marathon during the Spring of 2014. Then I aimed for a bigger goal. I wanted to complete a Marathon. I registered for the Philadelphia Marathon for the Fall of 2014. I started training for a full marathon but I did not get a chance to train well due to work and family commitments. The Philadelphia Marathon had an option. Runner could register for a full marathon but they had an option to complete just a half marathon and leave. I liked this option because I didn't have to commit to the full marathon if I wasn't able to do it. On the day of the race, I was hoping to run a full marathon but was not sure whether I could complete it.

When I reached my 13.1 miles, I felt strong and confident that I could finish the full marathon. I decided to complete the full 26.2 miles. I was fine until 19 miles. My foot started to hurt at the 19th mile. I put the blame on my new shoes and started walking. The next 6 miles looked like 16 with the foot injury. Then at around the 20th mile, I met a fellow runner who was almost my age and was also from NJ. She was a first time marathoner too. We were running and walking at the same pace. We started running and walking together. At one point she uttered, "Oh, thank you God, for sending Mani with me to complete this race". Miranda's company was so funny and helpful. She would spot the cameraman way ahead, and then would give me a warning to start running. As soon as the pictures were taken we would stop running and start walking. With these silly tricks the rest of the marathon became fun. We both finished the race together. Receiving the Marathon completion medal from the Philadelphia Mayor was very special. I will always cherish my first Marathon.

I was not happy with my time from my first Marathon. I blamed my foot injury for it. I registered for the NJ Marathon for the Spring of 2015 and started preparing. The initial part of my training went well and then I became swamped with work and had to work long and late hours. So I was not able to allocate enough time for the rest of the training. Five weeks before the race, I decided not to participate. Three weeks after my decision to not run, my work schedule relaxed little bit. I had time to prepare for the race 3 weeks the date. Just like at the Philly Marathon, the NJ Marathon has an option to leave at 13.1 miles. Once I reached 13.1 miles, I noticed only a few people were continuing. I wanted to become one of the few who finished and I did.

I then registered for the NYC Marathon through a Charity program. The Charity I was working with was Team for Kids. This charity help kids run and become athletic. I raised money and received an entry to run the prestigious marathon. The NYC Marathon is very different from the Philly and NJ Marathon in terms of the course path. We had to cross 5 bridges and multiple elevations. This was the toughest of all the three. The support from the NYC crowd was amazing. They stayed on the roads and cheered for amateur runners like me. That felt very special. As I write this chapter I have completed my second NYC Marathon. This Race had so many challenges and struggles. I like the challenge of the NYC Marathon and I'll be running it every year until I get mentally tired of running it.

I have completed 4 marathons and I'm not stopping there. I run these marathons to keep myself in good shape. I know only 1% of the population completes a marathon. The benefits of going the extra mile by completing marathons are many. I am in great shape. My confidence is high. My concentration level has improved a lot. I pay attention to details more than ever. I have a healthy BMI.

The effort of weeks of training to get ready for a marathon is the key to keeping my good health. Marathon training is one of the many examples of going the extra mile and reaping the rich rewards.

Conclusion

In all three of my personal stories, you might have seen the common thread that guaranteed my success was going the extra mile. If you want to guarantee your success, you need to follow *going the extra mile* principle. This is the only known way to attract money and the other good things that you want in life.

While learning the extra mile principle, it is important to learn the only formula that Napoleon Hill taught us in his legendary work.

$Q1 + Q2 + MA = R$

Q1 is the quality of service you render.

Q2 is the quantity of service you render.

MA is the mental attitude with which you render service.

R is the rewards you receive.

So, plan to provide the best possible quality of service in the maximum possible quantity, along with a positive attitude to enrich your customer or employer. This will lead to the maximum possible reward that you can attain.

Go the extra mile and follow the formula. You'll be guaranteed success in your life.

Mani Maran | Bio

Mani Maran's real-life story starts from a humble beginning. He was born in a small village at the interior part of South India. Through his hard work and efforts, he came to the US in 1994 to work as a software consultant. Though he was successful at his corporate work, when he ventured into business world, he was not so successful at it.

He owned and operated restaurants, apartment complexes, real estate investments and a web development business. He was forced out of all these businesses during the economic recession in 2009, and reached the lowest point of his financial life. But these failures taught him great lessons. He searched for answers as to how to develop success. He reached out to business coaches and studied self-revealing books and became Napoleon Hill Certified Instructor. These efforts helped him realize that success comes from within you."

CHAPTER 8

THRESHOLD LIMIT VALUE (TLV)

By Valen Vergara

Did you know that people only realize their limits, once they have pushed them? We all have something called resiliency ability. It is how we refrain from defeat, and make sure we keep on our goals and call them complete. This valuable skill set is also known as tolerance development. The threshold can be measured, and the higher the limit, the more valuable you will become because of it. This raises the question: What is your threshold limit value?

The threshold limit value (TLV) of a chemical substance is a level of which a worker can be exposed day after day for a working lifetime without adverse effects. A small percentage of the population learns to leverage this substance. This chemical make-up is the residue that coats the most successful performers on the planet. It holds a recipe for success and without it there is nothing left to do but quit. Self-limitations are bottled up by fear and conditioned by the six inches in between your ears.

I was once challenged to run a full marathon, with no training or experience under my belt. I had no idea that running a full marathon in this manner was an unusual practice. My mindset was very open to the notion, since deciding to do it was motivated by the need to win a bet. Be that as it may, I outperformed well past expectations and shocked the critics. It was only after receiving my medal and speaking with others following the event when I found out that what I did was quite the feat.

In hindsight, I found out that most people that get involved in running marathons start with ten kilometers, and then move up to the half marathon to prepare for the full marathon. However, if I were to have been privy to that information beforehand, I do not think I would have even attempted the run in the first place. I learned something important that day, and that was that I went the extra mile because I did not have any self-doubts. As a result, I was not only able to go the extra mile I was able to go twenty-six point two.

That fateful day, I unintentionally forced up my threshold limit value and raised the standard of my performance substance. I went so close to my breaking point that I almost went to the point of no return.

This process is merely a mechanism that can be activated by anyone at will. It is the mind at its finest. The greatest men and women in history have mastered this bodily function and have laughed in the face of fatigue. When you face your fear, the death of fear is certain and all that is left is momentum.

There was a double blind experiment done once based on Expectations Theory. In a classroom setting in San Francisco Bay, it was proven that the biases of teachers and their belief in their student's ability to perform, directly affected the student's success rates. The teachers in two separate classrooms were given fabricated representations of the students learning abilities. One class was labeled with an inferior intellect and the other was labeled as highly intellectual. Both classes ended up exactly as the teachers were told they would.

Correspondingly, one class performed very poorly, and the other class ended in excellence. All the students were chosen from a random sample for the experiment. This proved that the teachers self-fulfilling prophesy created the expected outcomes of the classrooms. It is like Henry Ford once said, "Whether you think you can or you think you cannot, you are right!"

There is a concept in psychology that involves the human predisposition to generate possible alternatives to something that has already happened. This is better understood as counterfactual thinking. Counterfactual thinking is what it states: "contrary to the facts."

These internal dialogues are made up of questions like, "what if?" and statements like "If I had only." Counterfactual thoughts are things that could never possibly happen in real-life because they solely pertain to events that have occurred in the past. This train of thought prevents people from going the extra mile in their business career and life.

It is the problems of the past and the anxiety of what the future may bring which adversely affects the most important thing of all, and that is the present time! The average human being will give up on the desired goal after three failed attempts. The reason we do this is because we are afraid to endure the feeling of not getting what we want. The fear of loss is painful and success is a habit of doing the right things.

In order to accomplish anything in the physical environment, we must go through a process of habituation at some level. Habituation is our sensory ability to normalize what we perceive as harmful stimuli from the environment. Let me prove it to you through an exercise.

First find a partner, and stand an arm's reach away from them. Then outstretch your arm and point your index finger above the participant's head. Then bring your pointed finger downwards between their eyes without touching their forehead, but close enough to warrant a reflex. Do that five times. What you will notice is that after the third or fourth time, the participant will no longer blink due to habituation. The participant has grown accustomed to the experience and has deemed the process non-threatening.

Whether it is minor or major, when you do what you fear the fear disappears! We are at times bounded by our rationality and when we unbind our mind from perceived stoppages we allow for breakthroughs. This is neuroplasticity of the brain, and when it comes to growth and development, what "fires together wires together!" Success is repetition, "the mother of all skill" and trying something new after a temporary failure.

Before we are going to be great at something, we are going to be good at it. Before we are going to be good at something we are going to be "not half bad" at it. Before that, we are going to be bad at it. Before that, we have to try! It is the sum of attempts that earns us our triumphs.

NEVER QUIT

"When things go wrong, as they sometimes will. When the road you're trudging seems all uphill. When the funds are low and the debts are high. And you want to smile, but you have to sigh. When care is pressing you down a bit. Rest, if you must, but don't you quit. Life is queer with its twists and turns, as every one of us sometimes learns. And many a failure turns about. When he might have won had he stuck it out. Don't give up though the pace seems slow—You may succeed with another blow. Often the goal is nearer than. It seems to a faint and faltering man. Often the struggler has given up. When he might have captured the victor's cup, and he learned too late when the night slipped down. How close he was to the golden crown. Success is failure turned inside out—The silver tint of the clouds of doubt. And you never can tell how close you are. It may be near when it seems so far. So stick to the fight when you're hardest hit—It's when things seem worst that you must not quit."

— Unknown Author.

Valen Vergara | Bio

VALEN VERGARA

Award Winning Entrepreneur. Asset Manager. Businessman. Developer. Humanitarian. International Bestselling Author. Columnist. Private Equity Investor. Trainer.

WWW.VALENVERGARA.COM

CHAPTER 9

HEALTH TO WEALTH - AN OVERLOOKED PATH TO SUCCESS

By Ray Cantu

"You can only love others as
much as you love yourself."

So, look in the mirror and ask yourself "How much do I love myself?"

Did you put junk food in your body this week? Did you exercise at least 30 minutes daily?

Do your actions reflect your self-love?

About seven years ago, I looked in the mirror and asked myself these same questions.

I was 30 pounds overweight and was not very happy in life. I wanted to be a Success but had no idea how to get there.

But I did know that my health was going to be a factor!

Over the last seven years, I have made my health a priority and EVERY aspect of my life has improved because of it. I have dropped the 30 pounds and proudly walk around with a chiseled body. I found the woman of my dreams and live a life I could have never imagined.

Now, I coach people to do what I did.

I partnered with a company called Beachbody, the leader in home fitness and nutrition, and have helped thousands of people get into the best shape of their lives.

And what I have seen is priceless.

The people that I have worked with have found the loves of their lives. They have opened new businesses and pursued their true callings in life. And they have found Success that has been hiding from them their whole lives.

It has been quite a surreal experience to see these coincidences unfold so many times over and over again.

And it was not until I completed my coursework as a Napoleon Hill Foundation Certified Instructor of the Science of Success that I realized what was happening.

So, if you have been searching high and low for Success to no avail, let me share with you the secret formula that I learned and how I can help you get there.

THE SECRET FORMULA

Napoleon Hill studied Success all his life and was able to discover commonalities in self-made legends such as Henry Ford, Thomas Edison, President Roosevelt and hundreds more.

What did he conclude?

Napoleon Hill determined that there are 12 True Riches of Life - Things that separated a truly successful person from others.

Most people have NO IDEA that there are 12 RICHES OF LIFE.

Can you name them?

Can you list their order of importance?

When society teaches us about success, it mostly entails a bunch of money and materialistic things.

But how many times have you seen a person with a bunch of money and things who does not seem gratified with life? Or very much liked by others?

Does that sound like Success?

I remember seeing an old bald headed man driving down the highway in a red convertible Mercedes with a hot babe in his passenger seat. He was extremely pale and very out of shape. He looked like he was one cheeseburger away from a heart attack.

Although he had a bunch of money, a nice car, and a hot date... Would you define that as Success?

I would not. And neither would Napoleon Hill.

Dr. Hill defined the 12 Riches worth pursuing as followed:

1. **Positive Mental Attitude**
2. **Sound Physical Health**
3. **Harmony in Human Relations**
4. **Freedom from Fears**
5. **Hope of Achievement**
6. **Capacity for Faith**
7. **Willingness to Share One's Blessings**
8. **Labor of Love**
9. **Open Mind on All Subjects**
10. **Self-Discipline**
11. **Capacity to Understand People**
12. **Economic Security**

Those are all listed in order of IMPORTANCE. Read them again!

Did you notice that Economic Security is LAST??

Where is it on your list?

And more importantly, where is SOUND PHYSICAL HEALTH on your list??

Are you putting your health on the back burner while you chase the almighty dollar? Maybe that's why you are not getting it. Have you thought about that?

What happens when you put your health first?

Well, that is what I want to talk to you about because I think it is important.

THE SCIENCE OF SUCCESS

As you may or may not know, Dr. Hill expanded on his *Think and Grow Rich* book with an actual course that anyone could follow. He broke Success down to a Science.

What does that mean?

It means that it works for anyone. All you have to do is follow the formula.

And whether you realized it or not, *GOING THE EXTRA MILE* is a big part of that formula.

In fact, Dr. Hill shared 17 Principles of Success and declared that only the first four are necessary. The other 13 are to expand on the first four.

Here are the 17 Principles:

1. **Definiteness of Purpose**
2. **Mastermind**
3. **Applied Faith**
4. **Go the Extra Mile**
5. **Attractive Personality**
6. **Personal Initiative**
7. **Positive Mental Attitude**
8. **Enthusiasm**
9. **Self-Discipline**
10. **Accurate Thinking**
11. **Controlled Attention**
12. **Teamwork**
13. **Learning from Adversity & Defeat**
14. **Creative Vision**
15. **Sound Health**
16. **Budgeting Time & Money**
17. **Cosmic Habitforce**

Did you see where *GOING THE EXTRA MILE* is?

It is FOURTH!!! One of the top principles to master!!

As a matter of fact, Dr. Hill has said,

> *"If I had to choose but one of the seventeen*
> *principles of success and rest my chances on*
> *that principle alone, I would, without*
> *hesitation, choose*
> *going the extra mile, because this is the*
> *principle through which one can make*
> *himself indispensable to others."*

So, let us talk about how you can GO THE EXTRA MILE with your health and fitness because I feel that when you concentrate your energy on this, the other riches in your life that you are pursuing will shortly follow.

Why?

Because you are putting in work to LOVE YOURSELF more. And when you LOVE YOURSELF more that means you can LOVE OTHERS MORE.

And BOOM.... just like that, the world's fortunes tilt in your favor.

A POWERFUL REALIZATION

I was in Alaska working as a summer camp counselor for a mission camp back in 2014 when I came to a biblical realization.

Whether you are religious or not, I think you can make the connection with this bible passage.

It comes from Matthew 22:34

> *"And when the Pharisees heard that Jesus*
> *had silenced the Sadducees, they themselves*
> *gathered together. One of them, an expert*
> *in the Law, tested Him with a question:*
> *"Teacher, which commandment is the*
> *greatest in the Law?"*

Jesus declared; 'Love the Lord your God with all your heart and with all your soul and with all your mind. This is the first and greatest commandment. And the second is like it: 'Love your neighbor as yourself. All the Law and the Prophets depend on these two commandments."

Now here is what I find interesting.

The Bible teaches us that God lives within us. That man has to search within to find God. That we all have the same creator and thus share common DNA.

> *"Don't you know that you yourselves are*
> *God's temple and that God's Spirit dwells*
> *in your midst?"*
>
> — Corinthians 3:16

So to love God…is really to love Yourself because He is in you.

And to love your neighbor as yourself means that you can ONLY love others as much as you love yourself.

WOW!!

Between the two, it is implied to LOVE YOURSELF.

What a realization!!

That to receive the true blessings in life, you must LOVE YOURSELF.

What if we spent the next 90 days working together on a better YOU? What would that do for your life?

What would happen if we made YOUR health a priority? Can you imagine the payout?

THE EXTRA BENEFITS OF GOOD HEALTH

Going the Extra Mile in your fitness will do more for you than you can imagine.

Think about it.

What happens when you drop 20 pounds?

Do you think your confidence will increase? Of course, it will, and that means you will tackle things that you have been avoiding and putting off.

Do you think you will smile more? Yes, you will, and that means more people will smile back!

Do you think your energy will increase? You betcha! And that means a more active life!

This is what Napoleon Hill refers to as the Law of Increased Returns.

Basically, it means that the work that you put in will pay back with a multiple of seven.

Can you see how the other Riches of life will be available when you focus on improving your health?

This reminds me of my good friend Adolf's journey.

Adolf had a great job, nice clothes and a very stable bank account. But his life was toxic.

His concept of Success was to have a stable family with good relationships with others. And he was so far from it that it was inconceivable for him even to believe possible.

His unhealthy habits of smoking cigarettes and drinking mass amounts of alcohol affected his relationships with himself, his friends and his coworkers.

He was a walking mess and was one DWI away from a long jail term. He was lonely, afraid and insecure.

Then one day, he decided to concentrate on his fitness. He was 40-pounds overweight when we started working together, and within six months, Adolf's life completely turned around.

He dropped those 40 pounds and completely eliminated the smoking and drinking from his life.

His newfound confidence propelled him to quit his job and relocate to a better support network where he found an even better job, a supportive church, and he has just had his first child.

What started as just one pushup, ended up being the catalyst he needed to find the success he wanted.

THE SOLUTION I PROMOTE

I think we can agree now that your health needs to be a priority.

But we have yet talked about HOW to win with your health and fitness goals.

So, let's lay out the basic *four* major principles of Success and how we will apply them.

1. <u>Definite of Purpose</u> - **Set a goal**

Success with your fitness is no different than success in other areas of your life. It ALL starts with setting a goal. We will work together to establish realistic goals and milestones. Each path is different, but the first step remains the same.

2. <u>Mastermind</u> - **Hire a coach and join a support group**

One of the first things we will do is schedule check-ins and unite you with others with similar goals. I have helped HUNDREDS of people to lose thousands of pounds and completely turn their health and fitness around 180 degrees. A true mastermind is composed of a group in complete harmony with the same goal. And my goal is to help you achieve your goal. We work together to make this happen.

3. <u>Applied Faith</u> - **Create a plan and take daily action**

Based on your goals, we will choose a health and fitness plan to follow. These are proven systems that hundreds of thousands have used to find success. We will start to track activity and consistency and let the scale and tape measure be our report card. My role is to believe in you until your own belief catches up...which IT WILL!!

4. <u>Go the Extra Mile</u> - **Do more than you think**

A big part of the journey are the intangibles like creating a fitness vision, setting up your workout areas, planning your meals and setting up personal barriers. I will show you the extra activities that you can do to guarantee you find success. We will succeed because we went the EXTRA MILE and covered the four pillars of Fitness Success - Fitness, Nutrition, Support and Prizes (be sure to ask me about these!)

GOING THE EXTRA MILE

This is a bit embarrassing to admit, but I have fallen for the gimmicks sold on TV infomercials.

It was a product called 6-second abs, and I truly believed that it was the solution to my problem of my jeans fitting too tight.

When it didn't work, I turned to the weight loss pills and quick fix diets.

Which to my surprise didn't work either.

What did work?

GOING THE EXTRA MILE!

Napoleon Hill defines *Going the Extra Mile* as doing MORE than you are paid to do.

He says that when you do, the universe is taking score and all that you put in will eventually be paid back out to you.

This concept is what is known as the **LAW OF COMPENSATION**.

And it is something I see violated over and over again with those in pursuit of healthier bodies.

Maybe you have experienced it yourself?

You follow a weight loss plan for a week and even manage to get to the gym a few days. And when the scale doesn't move, and you don't have an overnight six-pack...you give up.

That is if you don't know about the LAW OF COMPENSATION.

If you did then you WOULD NOT want Overnight Success.

You would gladly put in work day in and day out.

If you were on a mission to lose 20 pounds, then you would put in the work to lose 40!!!

When it comes to your fitness, there are several ways you can GO THE EXTRA MILE. Here are just a few.

1. Plan and prep your meals
2. Tape Your Fitness Goals everywhere
3. Create a Screen saver with your goal body type
4. Tell everyone you know about your fitness mission
5. Add a rep to each exercise set
6. Check in with your Support Group Daily
7. Invest in supplements
8. Hire a coach

MY OBSERVATION

My wife tells me all the time "How you do one thing is how you do EVERYTHING".

And how true that is!

We all know that life has valleys and peaks. Sometimes we feel like we are on top of the world and sometimes we feel like we are in a gutter.

Have you ever noticed how your activity levels are at those moments?

Remember that time you were depressed? Just seriously in the dumps. What was it like?

I would imagine that you became lazy. And you ate like crap.

Can you ever expect to get out of a hole like that?

It probably wasn't until you decided to snap out of it and do something…. anything… that you started to build momentum to get out of your funk.

Well, the same thing happens when you go the EXTRA MILE with your health and fitness.

You have ONE BODY! Just ONE!

If you take care of it, then it will take care of you.

And those habits that you build up will spread to all parts of your life.

Have you ever wondered why healthy and fit people seem to be happier?

There is no coincidence.

Napoleon Hill knew what he was doing in identifying Sound Health as the second most important RICHNESS to obtain.

NOW IS THE TIME

I am convinced that *GOING THE EXTRA MILE* with your fitness could be the ONE thing that catapults you into the stratosphere of Success.

I have made my profession helping people just like you obtain the True Riches of life as outlined by Dr. Napoleon Hill.

It is amazing to see the LAW OF INCREASED RETURNS take effect when one has applied *GOING THE EXTRA MILE* in their fitness.

Relationships improve. Fears are conquered. Self-Disciple is Mastered.

Can you see how these improved attributes can relate to Financial Gain?

I can attribute my Success to date to the decision I made to GO THE EXTRA MILE in my health and fitness.

Hopefully, I can share more of what I have learned with you in future encounters as your Beachbody Coach.

Until then...Be Healthy, Be Fit and LIVE LIFE!

Ray Cantu | Bio

Ray Cantu is a Certified Napoleon Hill Science of Success Instructor and a Star Diamond Beachbody Coach. He loves Surfing, Krav Maga, Salsa dancing and anything else that challenges his body. He has helped hundreds lose weight and get into great shape following a simple yet effective system. He saw his father's life cut short because of bad health habits and made it his mission to help others to not make the same mistakes. He works with people in all areas via internet and social media technologies. If you are looking for a solution for your health and fitness, then be sure to reach out to Ray. He is passionate about helping others get full control of their health so they can reach their full potential as high achievers.

Ray can be reached at 210.845.6849 or by email at ray@can2coaching.com. You can also find him on Facebook fb.com/coachraycantu or on his website: www.can2coaching.com.

CHAPTER 10

Going the Extra Mile Within

By Taylor Tagg

What Does Forgiveness Really Feel Like?

"I would have preferred that you would have protected me, loved me, and met my needs. But you didn't. So, I release the expectation that you ever would have protected me, loved me, and given me what I needed. I'm moving on with life now."

Those are the words (specific to your life) that begin the journey of forgiveness within and reconciliation of oneself to oneself. It's a journey into the mind, the heart, the physical body, and the spiritual realm, to free a person from the toxic ties that have binded them to another person in a negative way.

Walking the internal extra mile can carry benefits that reach beyond what one can perceive in the moment. New understanding, fresh energy, and a renewed sense of self begin to emerge after opening yourself to the process of internal cleansing.

Consequently, a person may feel lighter, and actually weigh less, after releasing themselves energetically from someone. Scientific studies have proven that people who were asked to release a resentment then jump into the air got off the ground a full 2 inches higher than those who were told to focus on a resentment and perform the same jump.

Forgiveness can literally make you lighter.

With so much to gain (or lose depending on how you look at it), why isn't releasing and forgiveness very popular today?

Because walking the extra mile within is scary.

If you give the hurt up (or rather heal it), what's on the other side? Does the other person go scot-free? If you open your heart, will you continue to hurt forever? Is forgiveness safe? These are legitimate concerns that a person gets fully answered as they go through the process of forgiveness.

Coming through the other side, most people come to realize that their own freedom never had anything to do with the other person's actions. One can separate their own need to hold another accountable for their behaviors from how they feel about those behaviors.

With this separation, one can release the pain. They also discover that the hurt does leave once it's simply processed in the body, mind, and heart. Forgiveness is safe and highly recommended for good health!

Let's look at the other side of the hurt. What if a person continues to feel robbed of joy the rest of their lives? Will one ever get over the feeling of being stuck? The answer to that is not until the energy of emotion is dealt with on the inside.

How do you deal with it? You feel.

You gather the courage to feel the hurt in combination with releasing your expectations and re-establishing your sense of personal boundaries. In a very short amount of time, the hurt begins to subside and then totally leaves as if it suddenly reached the finish line, received its trophy, and now is headed to its permanent vacation home away from you.

Emotions are simply energy...energy in motion that needs to move within the mind and body. When you hold on to negative energy, it gives the mind fuel for resentment and righteousness in the form of thoughts. The body, however, does not take kindly to stagnation or held energy.

After a period of time, the bottled energy turns toxic like spoiled milk and creates havoc within the body. Science has now proven that held energy can be detrimental to your health if held for extended periods of time. Once energy has been properly released, the body returns to its normal state of flow and movement.

I doubt there is a person on this planet that once he or she fully realized they were carrying the equivalent of spoiled milk within wouldn't try to throw it out immediately. A person just needs to know how to do it.

That's where I come in. A forgiveness coach helps one get rid of their spoiled milk once and for all and then work to build a better, stronger container.

A Session for the Ages

Mary came to me before my first forgiveness workshop and said, "I just want you to know, your workshop will change my life."

I replied, "Uh, OK," thinking yeah lady what kind of fruit loops did you have for breakfast?

However, I stayed open to the possibility that something good could come from it.

Mary had been the product of an alcoholic, abusive, non-present father and had not coincidentally married the same kind of man. She was physically sick and mentally "done" with life. She was 68 years old and had been carrying resentment in her heart towards her father for over 60 of those years.

Mary had reached the point where she intuitively knew that if she didn't do something different now, it would kill her. She felt like she had no choice but to forgive her father if she wanted to live.

During the course of the workshop, Mary was selected to demonstrate the forgiveness process for the rest of the group. This demonstration is for the benefit of all, to experience the Eight Steps of Freedom for themselves before they do it on their own.

Secondly, the demonstration is to help the selected volunteer free themselves with the help of the group. Great synergy is created when like-minded individuals become a person's cheerleader and prayer champion. Each person sends their energy and love to the person forgiven. This creates a tremendous sense of community and belonging for all involved.

As Mary continued with the process, what happened next was the stuff of legend.

I asked Mary to stand up and visualize an image of her father. Using her creative imagination, she saw him clearly sitting in a chair listening to her with full attention. Using her imagination was rather easy for Mary because she was dealing with her own painful memories of her father. As she saw dad in the chair, she gave him one of the most passionate, profanity-laced tongue-lashings I've heard in quite a while.

It was Level 10 stuff. She was pent up full of anger. Before we knew it, 60 years' worth of emotion came pouring out into the open.

She said, "How could you throw me away like the trash you Son of a Bitch! I'm the most precious piece of garbage you've ever been around. You wouldn't have survived if it wasn't for me. FUCK YOU old fart!"

The rage continued for twenty more minutes, until she was good and cleaned out with what she needed to say to the image of her dad. These internal stuck emotions are what I call the "emotional truth" that desperately needs to be verbalized and released from a person's being.

It's a chance for a person to say what was never said. In a controlled environment, one is free to put aside politeness and be as rude as they want to be because that is the truth that lies inside. It may be ugly, but it's the truth as that person knows and feels it.

It can be so freeing to say what was always underneath, to verbalize what was felt but never had the opportunity to be relinquished.

Mary proceeded to release the expectations she had of her father, one by one. She released the expectation that her father would have protected her, would have been kinder, would have chosen her over the alcohol, would have realized how sick he truly was, and would have loved her the way she needed as a child. She kept going with each expectation until they were all gone.

It's amazing how once a person verbalizes their preferences of others, they realize just how many ways they expected them to behave.

Once Mary was ready to move on from her expectations, I had her again use creative imagination to see and feel a bubble of colored light all around that would bathe her from head to toe in warmth and healing, helping her to also establish her sense of personal boundaries that hadn't existed for many years.

Seeing her father as separate from her, she opened up to the Universe to provide her what her father never could...a sense of belonging, purpose, and unconditional love from her Creator. Mary also sent her father a piece of her own love for his healing in his own time.

As we winded down the demonstration, Mary saw the good in her father and verbalized it.

"I release you to be you dad. I release me to be me. And I release me from you."

Mary sat in silence for a few minutes, grateful for the wonderful opportunity to forgive and create a new path in her life.

It was an unforgettable hour. The group rushed in to give Mary long hugs and well wishes. Many people were stunned, crying, and cheering her new freedom all in the same breath.

Quite frankly, I was amazed. I was floored by Mary's conviction, passion, and courage to go the extra mile and grieve the loss of her father the way she wanted him to be.

Mary charted a new course that day for the better. She hasn't been the same since. She was right. The workshop truly did change her life.

Mary has attended almost every one of my forgiveness workshops since that day, lovingly lending her experiences and praying for others to gain their freedom and heal their souls.

Mary's physical and mental health returned as well. Best of all, Mary can now say no if it means protecting herself or the good health she deserves.

The workshop group witnessed a miracle in Mary's courage to rid herself of her spoiled milk and make room for fresh, new life to enter her body, mind, and heart.

If people only got an advanced sample of the blessings and refreshment that were waiting for them on the other side of releasing and forgiving, they would sign up for the Eight Steps to Freedom in droves.

Like the wise men of old once said, "What appears to be weakness is actually strength in disguise."

Changing the Future of the Family

Today, the secrets of forgiveness are held by the courageous. What if the magic answers in life were about unlearning, undoing, letting go, forgiving, and releasing our childhood hurts, rules, and paradigms that were supposedly meant to protect us?

What if a person who grew up learning their family's dysfunctional patterns decided one day that those patterns will end with them?

What if you could set a new direction for the legacy of your children, grandchildren, great grandchildren and generations to come?

Guess what? You still can.

Opening to and becoming aware of what is keeping you trapped in resentment, hurt, blame, guilt, and shame is the first step to ending the circle of sadness in your life.

It also starts by becoming the example by gathering the courage to forgive and set yourself free.

Imagine your family suddenly wondering why you seem brighter even though they may not be able to figure out why. By walking the extra mile within, you set a loving example that many generations will follow because they need freedom from their hurts too.

That example can be you.

There isn't a day that goes by where I don't thank the Lord for blessing me with the opportunity to help others forgive and find peace.

It's the most precious gift I have ever received in life.

The beauty of forgiveness leaves me in awe every time I witness it. A person that can open to their own vulnerability will make amazing things happen.

The problem is we don't want to get vulnerable. Yet there is ultimate freedom smack dab in the middle of that vulnerability. It's the getting there that scares us to death.

When one finds the courage to open their heart, the bet pays off and all the cards come up aces. You will be rewarded for your efforts. Nature demands a return for struggle.

Napoleon Hill summed it up best, "The time will never be 'just right.' Start where you stand, and work with whatever tools you may have at your command, and better tools will be found as you go along."

Godspeed to your healing and renewal.

Love and forgiveness be with you always.

Taylor Tagg

ForgiveandFindPeace.com

Taylor Tagg | Bio

Taylor Tagg has a passion for helping people breakthrough barriers and resolve internal conflicts. He is a Forgiveness Expert and the author of four personal development books Enrich Your Sunrise, The Path to a Peaceful Heart, Adversity to Advantage (co-author), and Refusing to Quit (co-author). Taylor is also an international speaker on the topics of Emotional Intelligence, Trauma, Forgiveness, and Overcoming Adversity.

At the heart of Taylor's work is assisting people in becoming the healthiest version of themselves. In addition to twenty years of Corporate Experience at AutoZone, ServiceMaster, and FedEx, Taylor is a Certified Leadership Instructor of the Napoleon Hill Foundation and a Certified Forgiveness Coach and Facilitator from the Midwest Institute for Forgiveness Training. He is also a contributing writer to The Good Men Project and The Huffington Post.

Credentials:

Certified Forgiveness Coach & Facilitator

Certified Leadership Instructor – Napoleon Hill Foundation

Certified Career Readiness Instructor

Specialty Training in Psychosynthesis

Specialty Training in Strategic Intervention Coaching

Specialty Training in PTSD, Anxiety, and Stress Related Traumas

CHAPTER 11

Michael's Story: A Story of a Greek Immigrant

By Stella Tartsinis

Life has a tendency to be filled with twists and turns, upward hills, roadblocks, and unforeseeable situations that hit your soul so powerfully it motivates the will into action. We cannot anticipate or foresee the calculation needed to strategize efforts to meet life's demands and challenges. Sometimes you have no choice but to go the extra mile to ensure a life of fulfillment and prevent poverty.

From the beginning, we are taught through social heredity that we need to play it safe, be careful, do what is required, stay above water, do what you are told to do, amongst many other limiting phrases. Society likes playing it safe, and cringes at the word "effort" because more effort is needed when we come upon failure. When we are falling behind, people tell us to put more effort into our work. On the other hand, greater effort can lead to an incredible life full of fantastic opportunities.

Born to Go the Extra Mile

Michael was born in Kavala, Greece in 1939. His father was a police officer and his mother stayed home raising four boys. He grew up in a time in Greece where numerous political upheavals and wars overtook the country, resulting in World War II battles and Greece's Civil War in 1946 - Communist Greeks versus the Democratic Greeks.

He grew up when *Going the Extra Mile* was used to ensure the survival of the Greek people. The Greco-Italian War on October 28,

1940, resulted in the Greek Prime Minister Metaxas standing his ground, refusing to surrender to the Italian forces. He responded with "Oxi" (meaning "No"). The day the Greeks said "Oxi" was the day Greece entered World War II. In 1942, Greeks adopted this day as a day of celebration for standing their ground refusing to surrender and doing whatever it took to ensure ownership of their country. Going the extra miles was the mindset of the Greek people of that time.

Prominent leaders have praised Greeks for Going the Extra Mile, giving selfless service for the good of humanity. Winston Churchill wrote that "Greeks do not fight like heroes; heroes fight like Greeks," while President Franklin Roosevelt said; "When the entire world had lost all hope, the Greek people dared to question the invincibility of the German monster raising against it the proud spirit of freedom."

The world witnessed the power or the spirit of the Greek people's fight against the Axis Forces (Rome, Berlin, and Tokyo). Greeks fought vigorously even though they lost the last battle. Adversity provided lessons in backbone development for the Greek people, strengthening their spirit, and the spirit of future generations.

Growing up in with his country's challenges, Michael had the mind of the Greek people in his make-up, which is a vision that stands up for righteousness. The world endured tremendous hardships in World War II, but Greeks would subsequently face tougher times with their civil war.

The Death of Michael's Father

In 1948, life was never the same again for Michael's family. His father died at the age of forty from stomach cancer. His mother was left to raise four boys ages 5 to 13, on her own, during a turbulent time in Greece's history. Fortunately, the family had a few housing units to support them during those difficult years, but even then, it was not easy. Something happened inside the four boys when they lost their father at their tender young ages while living in Greece's toughest times. Perseverance and the need to go the extra mile was defined in the family living without a father during some of the most difficult times in Greece's history.

Definite Major Purpose Found through an Apprenticeship

At the age of twelve, just three years after the death of his father, Michael entered into an apprenticeship with a master carpenter and molder. Throughout his youth, he worked every day with this master carpenter instead of pursuing a high school education. Michael spent time with this master carpenter learning the art of making furniture and building homes. This skill was a blessing because Michael found his Definite Major Purpose. He loved working with wood, and eventually became good enough to leave the apprenticeship to work on his own. He began working on various projects for clients. He started building a name for himself in Kavala.

The Entrepreneurship

As the years went by, he acquired enough experience and funds to start his own business. He applied his specific carpentry knowledge and organized its use to build a furniture company in the early 1960's. The furniture company was a partnership with a friend and they worked together in a mastermind alliance.

By *going the extra mile*, Michael worked hard developing his furniture company into a thriving business. He taught his employees how to use the machinery, craft furniture, and build quality products by embodying most minute details. *Going the Extra Mile* brought rewards as customer orders were plentiful, making his furniture business one of the most successful companies in Kavala. All his hard work paid off.

As time passed, life brought its blessing to Michael. In 1966, he married the daughter of a neighbor who rented an apartment from his family. The next year, their first daughter Anna was born. Life couldn't be better. The riches that they enjoyed living in a beautiful house with its interior made of marble flooring, Corinthian-styled columns, and the finest furniture from his company, as well as plenty of other items. Anna had room to play and run around enjoying a prosperous life. She had a pony, a backyard, and toys were abundant. Life in Kavala could not be any better.

Adversity Knocking at the Door

A couple of years later, in 1968, adversity knocked on Michael's door. His wife had a miscarriage, losing her baby boy. The loss of this child was a big disappointment to Michael because he wanted to have a son so badly. The next year, they had a healthy baby girl. The beginning of life's twists and turns started to unfold, as the next decade of life would put him on a roller coaster ride showing how life can push you so hard that every time you get up, you just fall right back down again and again.

Shortly after their second daughter was born, Michael had an accident at the furniture company. Accidently, his three fingers were sawed off while working on a project with a saw cutter. This accident was the beginning of the storm in his life. He was not on good terms with his partner at this point. Through many arguments, things moved from bad to worse. Shortly after he lost three fingers in his right hand, the furniture company burned down to the ground.

When adversity enters through the door, it is faced, and sometimes overcome. Michael's plan was to rebuild the furniture company himself. Unfortunately, the business went bankrupt resulting in a tremendous debt owed to the Greek government. The writing was on the wall and a big decision had to be made to find a way out of this circumstance. Somehow when adversity appears, so does going the extra mile. *Going the Extra Mile* is like a soldier combatting the enemy. Michael knew this and embraced *Going the Extra Mile* out of necessity.

Start Where You Stand!

At this point in his life, he had a wife, two small children, and a destroyed business. It was at this time that the crossroads became visible. Michael would have to make a decision that would change the course of his life forever. This decision was the turning point where lessons from his other self or inner self were learned. This experience was compounded with stress knowing that many obligations were pulling on him. Having a family with no means of financial support was quite stressful. His possessions and home were his only assets now. He had to make serious decisions and take decisive action. He had to start again where he stood!

Michael owed a tremendous debt to the Greek government from his bankrupted business. At that time, if a debt was not paid promptly, jail was the alternative. Jail time was not an option for Michael! He chose to sell every possession, and immigrate to the United States of America. Neither he nor his wife knew a word of English. They had to learn English from the University of Hard Knocks. The family relocated to the United States, and Michael had no means of supporting them. At this point, his three brothers were already living in the United States. His brothers sponsored Michael and his family so that entry into the United States, and obtaining a green card, was possible.

In 1972, Michael was a legal alien living in the United States, having no employment and not able to speak a word of English. Knowing that he could never return to Greece until the debt was paid in full was emotionally difficult. Greece was his homeland, where he once was successful, having the perfect life just a few years prior to his immigration to the United States. Now living in a new country without a dime in his pocket, he had to find employment to support his family.

Humility Comes Knocking at the Door

His youngest brother owned a diner in East Windsor, Connecticut where he employed Michael as a dishwasher. This was all that he could do since he just recently immigrated to the United States with his young family, with seven of his fingers, and not knowing a word of English. People recommended that he enroll in the food stamp program, but his pride refused such a suggestion, and resulted in turning on more will power through going the extra mile.

He worked for a few years as a dishwasher at his brother's restaurant while living with his second oldest brother and his wife in their apartment. Working as a dishwasher was a huge blow to Michael's ego. He was one of the best woodworkers and molders in Greece, had his own successful company, and just like that, he quickly lost everything in a few years. He recalled where he currently was realizing his current condition, but he also had a vision of where he wanted to go just as he did when he built his first business in Greece.

He eventually moved his family to an apartment near his bothers residence. Life was getting better only because he began to network and build contacts in the Greek community. His talents were noticed, bringing in multiple referrals. Carpentry was his one skill, his Definite Major Purpose. He worked as a carpenter fulfilling a variety of jobs to support his family. He worked long hard hours alone, not hiring any employees so that he could save money faster. Going the Extra Mile was certainly not easy, but it was necessary to defeat and avoid a life of poverty. Time with the family was mostly put on hold during these tough years. He reserved the weekends mostly for spending time with his family, but sometimes that was not possible.

He was starting to build his carpentry business working on restaurant interiors mainly in the Greek community. He began to build homes working as a contractor on house projects. Fate certainly started to turn around, but in order to sustain and benefit from the work orders coming in, he had to go the extra mile working long hours on his own. There would be times that he would work himself into exhaustion, needing to recover by sleeping during the day.

Going the Extra Mile became his way of life, which was motivated by having to find the means to survive in a foreign country. He finished each job with extra details, keeping to the *Going the Extra Mile* mindset. He would decorate the wooden borders on the walls, the wooden booths, and the door arches with the finest detail. He made sure that all his clients were satisfied with the job, and readily available for any alteration even though he may have been in the middle of other jobs. His going the extra mile resulted in many referrals. Work was good, his English was getting better and the children were getting louder. Yes, louder! Especially the second daughter who loved playing outside, and running around in the small two-bedroom apartment.

In1976, Michael had a new addition to the family, a baby boy. His wish of having a boy was fulfilled. He may have been head over heels with happiness, but the neighbors in the apartment felt quite the opposite with the new addition to the family. His neighbors had issues with the noise levels of his family; a loud infant, and an energetic toddler making the noise intolerable. The cops even paid a couple of visits to his family because of neighbor complaints. The family saw this trouble coming from a mile away realizing that they would need to act fast to move into a house.

In 1978, Michael purchased property and built his own home in Somers, Connecticut. It was a three-bedroom house in a rural part of the state. Everyone was happy, including the neighbors in the apartment complex and his family. As fate would have it, life was changing for the better.

After many years of carpentry work, Michael decided to venture into a different career path. He decided to become a developer of commercial real estate. Michael decided to retire his laboring carpentry work to metamorphosis into his new Definite Major Purpose. At that time in the early 1980's, purchasing real estate was more affordable than in our present time of 2016. He took advantage of the lower cost of property by using his home as collateral to secure a business bank loan to purchase land and the needed funds for starting his commercial real estate business.

He went the extra mile when he took a risk to start a new business using his home as collateral. He took a chance *Going the Extra Mile* to organize his business. *Going the Extra Mile* sometimes means taking a risk. Every time we go the extra mile, there is no guarantee of immediate payment of services rendered, but that is not to say that payment will be withheld indefinitely. At some point, there is a reward for the efforts made as the Universe pays in full at the right time.

Building the Second Business

In the early 1980's, the economy was starting to recover and in 1983 there was economic growth in the United States under the Reagan Administration. This was the time that Michael built his first strip mall. His business was going well so he kept building new strip malls in pairs – two adjacent strip malls on each property. He wanted to expand what he had and realized that furthering his business gave him a goal to always be moving forward growing his business. *Going the Extra Mile* focuses on forward movement and striving for excellence. By rendering more service, it allows growth and achievement of miraculous goals. He expanded his business into other towns. He totaled five strip malls by the end of the 1980's.

Besides building a commercial real-estate business he financed a few restaurants in his shopping centers. He established partnerships as a financier of a Chinese restaurant, a family pie restaurant, and a pizzeria restaurant named after his second daughter.

Waves of Health Impediments

Stress and worry have consequences that result in sickness. The earlier struggles and worries to build a business had caused a tremendous strain on Michael's body.

In 1984, the family heard a loud thump upstairs in the bathroom, and when Michael's wife checked on what caused the sound, she saw him lying down next to his own pool of blood. Michael suffered a bleeding ulcer that, if it weren't for his brother convincing him to go to the hospital, he would have died from blood loss. He had to spend a week in the hospital for the necessary recovery time. After he healed from the ulcer, he continued working, but made more mindful choices to reduce stress and worry from his state of mind.

In 1992, the struggling economy affected Michael's business to the point of almost losing everything. Through worry, and despair came hope as though a beam of light burst from the dark. His brother-in-law in Germany came to his assistance to loan him one hundred thousand dollars to refinance his business. If it were not for his brother-in-law, he would have lost his business.

In 1994, Michael was at his office, and felt discomfort in this chest that continued in cycles. This pressure in his chest was a heart attack. When the ambulance brought him to the hospital, he had to have immediate heart surgery. Michael had to stay about a week in the hospital, and many more weeks to recover from his heart surgery at home. At that time, his son was starting to take care of the business. Michael had no choice but to place the responsibility of the business onto his son.

In 2004, ten years later, Michael was back in the hospital. This time he was administered into the hospital for possible pneumonia. The doctors discovered artery blockages that required a triple bypass to fix the problem.

Since then doctors have monitored his health. His health conditions were influenced greatly by his state of mind. Living a life of worry and stress resulted in a series of health issues. After he had given all of his authority to his son to manage the business, he had achieved peace of mind. From this point on, a full retirement from any business dealings was implemented. Living a retired life allowed him to engage in peaceful activities such as hunting, fishing and spending time with friends. He was enjoying other riches in life, eight grandchildren who would visit, friendships, and a life free from worry.

Takeaways from Michael's Story

1. Adopt a Definite Major Purpose such as a skill. Michael had carpentry, and synthesized it into a business. He took carpentry and business and the outcome was a commercial real estate developer. How can you synthesize what you do to create additional forms of income?
2. Learning from Adversity. Michael learned that when adversity comes along more effort was required to ride the storms of adversity into success. He had the pressure of having a young family, which required *Going the Extra Mile* to ensure a live away from poverty.
3. *Going the Extra Mile*. We learned from the Greek's spirit that you put all that you have into what you do to overcome defeat. *Going the Extra Mile* is motivated by adversity and also by passion. He went the extra mile first out of his passion for carpentry, and secondly, out of adversity.

How to develop Going the Extra Mile Mindset

When you are overcome by defeat, use effort by *going the extra mile*. You develop the *Going the Extra Mile* mindset by analyzing what you want in life and making sure that you put more effort than most to stick out from others around you. We are brainwashed through social heredity with the word "average" as being good or an accomplishment. Why be average when you have a chance to be great! *Going the Extra Mile* allows for greatness to unfold from average. Average may be your starting point, but greatness can be yours by going the extra mile. Make this the aim in your life.

My father Michael

Michael is my dad, and even though this is my father's story, it also is who I am. I was brought up through his challenges in life, and have seen this story with my own eyes. My dad, told me when I wanted to give up, that I am not a person who gives up. When I was down in college one year, my Dad told me to come home. When I have any difficulties in life, Dad is always there.

As a child, I saw the strength in my father's spirit. He did not sit down and let life give him what life wanted, but instead, he stood up and told life what he would accomplish. Even at the end of his career, life did not take him down despite business failures, a near bankruptcy, and multiple health issues. Michael passed the baton over to his son to continue what he spent years developing.

Michael was born in 1939, and implemented "Oxi" ("No") Day of 1940 to his life. "Oxi" to failure, "Oxi" to complacency, and "Oxi" to defeat. Why not adopt an "Oxi" Mindset to your life? When you are down, say "Oxi" and get up and tackle life with *Going the Extra Mile*.

Stella Tartsinis | Bio

Stella Tartsinis is a speaker, educator, musician, and U.S. Soldier. She is a motivational leadership speaker on the topic of teamwork, Peak Performance and the Psychology of Selling. She is an advocate of design thinking to motivate ideas in teams. Her message is to always to go the extra mile, moving away from average into the creative zone where designing your life becomes a reality through Peak Performance habits and teamwork.

She holds a Doctorate of Musical Arts from Rutgers University, and performs in New York City. She has performed music in various venues including Carnegie Recital Hall, and as a Broadway pit musician. She has been an educator in the New York City Department of Education system for the last ten years. In the Army Reserve, her current rank is a staff sergeant, serving since 2002. She has been serving in the capacity of an Army musician in historical events such as Pope Benedicts farewell visit to the United States ceremony with Vice President Cheney in attendance, re-opening of the Statue of Liberty, as well as many performances for diplomats and dignitaries.

Stella is a motivational leadership speaker who brings in her army leadership experience with a twist to her speaking. She has been an Army musician since 2002, and as a military musician, she uses both leadership and creativity for innovation and problem solving. Stella has attained a Doctorate in Musical Arts degree from Rutgers University. She speaks of the habits she developed from childhood that she consistently practiced to become a professional musician. Stella is a Certified John Maxwell Speaker, Coach, and Trainer.

She has been an educator for 12 years in the New York City Department of Education system where she learned how to apply the latest assessment tools to calculate, adjust and refine growth in learners. From her Napoleon Hill certification training, she has gained extensive knowledge of both *Think and Grow Rich* and the 17 Principles of Personal Achievement". Success is consistency, persistence, specific aims and goals.

Stella can be reached at stella@stellatartsinis.com

CHAPTER 12

The Reciprocations of Life

By Brandon Tyus

et me have my million dollars! Better yet, just give me enough money so I no longer have to worry about my bills, because as soon as get enough I want to give and help all the people I can. We all have hearts for giving; how do you give when you just don't got? Many of our giving's come to a screeching stop, because we look at what we have in belief that it is just not enough. Somewhere out there we feel entitled to amounts we have not established worth for. How can you get a million dollars putting in a penny's worth of work? The two questions seem synonymous, revealing each other and their flaws. To receive the penny, you go the mile that has been directed for you to go. On the other side, to receive the million dollars you go the extra mile nobody expected you to go.

Going the extra mile is not to meant to be a perfectionist, doing better than what everyone else is doing, but to be better than what you did yesterday as perfection is a myth and progression is the goal. It is the very principle that sets the majority of natures' laws into effect to work either in your benefit, or, if neglected, to your detriment. Napoleon Hill and his viewpoints are sound through experiment of not only him, but countless people who have accepted the challenge of following his philosophy even after his passing. They are just as effective today as they were we he first created them. He not only created an abundant life for himself, but came up with a system dependent blueprint that now enables any and everybody to do the things they wish to attain, and acquire it! The most prominent quote picked up from Dr. Hill is "whatever you do to, or for another person, you do to, or for yourself multiplied in kind."

Dr. Hill's first book *Think and Grow Rich* has sold over 100 million copies, and the number one thing that needs to be brought to its attention is starting with the title itself. The title is named "*Think and Grow Rich*", it does not state "Do and Grow Rich" as many of us do the most we can and work very hard and honest lives only to come up short with the same repeating problems on a day to day basis. After a while times like that get hard. Nobody likes to get beat up, torn down, and constantly told "no" when it comes to their truest desires. We do so much, but the irony is that when we wake up we will do something regardless. Honestly, even when we die we will still do something. Grant it, the only thing we can do at that point is change to dust, but the fact of the matter is that we will always be doing something. That is just the laws of nature. Nothing can be recreated or destroyed. So with that being said, it is not necessarily what we do that is the deciding factor on what we get. It is what we think when we get out of bed. It is actually what we think that gets us out of bed to begin with.

When someone has the desire to make *going the extra mile* a habit. It is not the action that they make a habit first, but the thought of doing more for someone or something that drives the body to do more. Before any physical habit can manifest there must be habit in thought. Creating a physical habit, before the thought habit is like placing the cart in front of the horse. It will look good in the beginning, but eventually that horse is going to move, and it will be in the opposite direction you want it to go in. Leaving your vision to grow smaller and smaller until you lose sight of it, and either forget about it or become so discouraged that you want to forget about it. A temporary fix is just the opposite of going the extra mile. To allow the principle of going the extra mile to work for you it must be consistent in thought of how you can better someone's life. Do not do a little more than what was expected, one time, and expect the world to give you abundance.

The concept of *going the extra mile* is taking your eyes off of yourself and focusing on the bettering of your mate, your peers, your community, your workplace, etc. It is reversing the thought process from "what's in it for me?" to "what can I give of me?" For so long our thoughts have been trained to program our minds that we must get before we can give. It has been made logical for us to think in terms of "once I have everything I need, then I can help others get what they need." Although, logical in sight, it is irrational in nature. Let us turn to nature for proof. Bees leave out of their hives going to countless flowers pollenating them, serving their purpose as being natures gardeners ensuring the flowers are properly groomed to grow healthy and sustain the intended lifespan. The bee's actual desire is not to nurture the plants, but to receive the honey they get out of serving the plants. Nature has set herself up to be a performance-based eco system. If we were to follow bees through their quest of getting honey you will never see a bee go out; serve one or two flowers, then come back and rest all day. They have an expectation of how much honey they want, so they make sure the worth of their work is in direct proportion to their desire. Encouraging the bees to be out all day pollenating hundreds of flowers to be sure they will reap the rewards they intend on receiving. The bees know by doing the best it can for the flowers, in return the flowers will provide the best they can for the bees. Now, imagine if bees had the same power we as humans do with the capacity to think consciously and decided to neglect this nature they follow by. Expecting honey first before they went out and served the flowers. Something as little as a bee can completely devastate the entire eco system.

Although, we are much more complex and powerful than a bee the same basic concept resides. In broad terms, life is a reflective nature. What we or anything else give out, we all must get back, but before we get back we must give out. Which makes it impossible for us to ever have enough to give to anyone, if we are trying to put giving on hold, and receive the getting back portion, first. The irony of this concept is when your giving is on hold, your receiving is also on hold. This is the perfect example to show why people never win, and believe that life is terrible. We have to realize that we receive our terrible circumstances of scarcity and poverty, because we are scarce in our giving to life. We provide little in charity, do just enough to get by at work, put minimal effort in pleasing our spouse, and family, do poorly in our service to others, and the best reason we have for our actions is that they did not do it first, or maybe you did it one time and they did not appreciate the service you gave them so you never did it again. We have all been at these points at some time or another, through our lack of knowledge in nature we fail to see what we do, in the attempt, to hurt them we hurt ourselves.

Going the extra mile works both positively and negatively. A very vivid picture has been drawn out as to what can happen if you decide to neglect this principle, or possibly wonder why problems continue to surface ending with you not getting what you desire. There was a time when I was constantly wondering why I was getting the same reoccurring problem in my life. These problems kept happening until I made a decision for change and started applying the extra mile. It was when I was eighteen I just graduated high school, and I could not keep a home to save my life. I had not lived with my mother since I was sixteen as it seemed that, that would be the best option for me, and I had no choice but to do my best in finding a place to sleep when I got out of work. Whether, if it was on a park bench, a friend's car backseat, or, there were a couple times, even paying security to stay inside of a college building. I didn't have much money, because I was out spending my money in places it had no business going. I never could get a loan from people, and I think about it today and it was because I wouldn't do them any favors. I did not want to provide worthy service that I knew I was not going to get paid for, right away. It turns out that my pay would have come at the points of need if I was willing to help when they asked.

I was stuck in the mindset of putting my giving on hold until I had enough for myself to feel comfortable giving. I was stuck in this rut of always feeling sorry for myself, convincing myself that I should get before I got. I did not believe in free work, or doing more than what I was paid to do. That was the thought habit I held for quite some time, and it eventually put me in a position where I could seal my convictions. Since life is a reflective nature, I started finding myself around people with the same mentality, always feeling sorry for themselves; giving little worth, but expecting much more pay. We indulge in conversations of what we feel we deserved, and what wasn't right. The only difference between them and I was that they had a home to go to, and I did not. They had a promised meal, and I did not. Sure, they would help for a little bit, but again they shared the same mentality I had. They did not believe in help without pay and started asking me, essentially, what was in it for them if my stay was too long. I found myself going down a rabbit hole and the light was growing more and more dim, and my life of success was fading away.

I realized that I had to do something different; blaming others was getting me anywhere, but down a deeper hole. So I had to find a way to get what I wanted, which was a foundation. I didn't say home, because along with the home there were many problems I had to take care of physically, spiritually, mentally, and emotionally. Although, buying a house was going to provide me shelter that doesn't always mean that I am guaranteed a home. During my journey of trying to find a way of how to build this foundation, an older man walked passed me and out of nowhere. The old man starts talking to me and says the only way to receive is to give, and I looked at him in disbelief. He said nothing more, but did something I would never forget. He lifted his hand and positioned it into a fist, and told me to give him something. I looked and told him I couldn't, and he would not be able to hold on to it anyway. His eyes got big, and told me that this was how I was trying to receive myself, and that the same hand that receives is the same hand that gives, and he walks away. When the man left it was the turning point of my life. It was great timing, because by that time I was running out of places to go. During this time, I was working at Wendy's, and the next day I went in for work and all I kept thinking was how could I give to receive more. I opened my mind to the concept keeping my hand open. Not a moment passed a coworker of mine was complaining that she had to work a double, but really wanted to go to a party. The comment landed on me like a ton of bricks, and I immediately spoke up and said that I would take the shift. With pure happiness she thanks me, and assisted me the entire shift ensuring that I had everything that I needed. Something that a coworker had never done for me before. Even before the extra services she gave me. I actually felt really good that I was able to help someone be happy, in turn it made me happy.

At that moment, I seen the older man with his fist, in my mind, and it started to open up and I understood on such a deep level that when the day ended, I wasn't as tired as I usually was. I even stayed up longer in awe of that fact that I didn't have any money to give. However, I still had something to give and it was my services. It was my ability to do more than what any expected of me, and nobody told me I had to do it. I did it myself, and she paid me back not only in more time at work to get paid, but more help to make my workday easier. The little worth I had given, gave back a huge return of reward. The next day, I was excited to see whom else I could help.

I soon found myself taking a shift off of someone's hand every day; worked a double every shift. I was loving the feeling I was getting because of the smiles I kept getting. On top of the fact that more and more people wanted to help me. I started getting free food. When I left out of work I came across a friend who was so loving at heart, and was heartbroken about my position; decided to help me. From that point on I had a place I could go to, to sleep at night. I started finding more ways to help along with my coworkers I started making the customers smile. I became so ambitious, I started to laugh at myself, because it was all for a smile, but what really instilled this feeling of fulfillment in me was that I was the reason these people were smiling. Nobody told me I had to do these things, but in my heart I knew the worthy service I was giving was only going to make a better life for me. In my eyes it had no choice, if I was creating a better life for the people around. The friends I was once hanging out with started to fade, I got a raise at Wendy's and even came across a customer who enjoyed the experience so much that he offered me a better paying job with more happy people! I marveled at what was happening in my life.

From there, I have had one of the grandest paths as one opportunity led to another, and I built on the opportunity a foundation of giving. From my thoughts, internally, of how I could give of myself led to, externally, what people now want to give to me. Nature had reflected my thoughts and intention into my physical reality. I am now 22 with a thought habit so deeply ingrained of how I can give, it has heightened my creativity, supplied me with more energy, given me more confidence in myself, and a whole flock of friends with great hearts and a servant mentality, including the friend that I met during those dark times. Since I have made this a habit, life has given me a house I have always imagined, three cars, and even a cleaning lady that comes every Thursday. Thinking back to my time at Wendy's my job never changed, my coworkers stayed the same, there was no dramatic event that occurred. Everything stayed the same, but my thinking. As soon as I changed my thinking and redirected my focus it put me in a position that propelled me to better places than I thought I would actually get to. Life will always and forever be reflective in its nature. I found this out during times that were unfavorable. Sometimes we must be put in hard positions to discover thoughts we would have never had if the event had not made us struggle. If we do the best we can in life, life will always do the best it can for us. It is a law that cannot be broken, nor lifted for anyone. Now anytime I want something, I give it first.

So if you want money, give something to charity. If you want a friend, become friendly to people. If you want help figuring out a problem, go out and help someone else with their problems. To become rich in our lives we must go out and enrich others in theirs. Going the extra mile gives you so many more benefits than just money; people who do not go the extra mile completely miss out. The most important thing you get is fulfillment, giving feeds the soul as, Dr. Hill, would say. It is what fills you up inside and that feeling has no price tag that can ever match it. Following this habit builds a positive mindset overall. You must be in a positive frame of mind to be able to help someone else turn a negative situation into a positive. Helping someone do so without positivity, is like laughing without a smile on your face. Either impossible, or very difficult to do. I am so confident that I challenge you to laugh in the mirror without smiling and see if you can actually do it.

Doing the best you can in life builds spiritual credit that cannot be seen, but is always rewarded. Nobody needs to see anybody do a good deed, because the person that is doing it will know the reason they did it for. What is done in secrecy will be rewarded in public. *Going the extra mile* has endless benefits. They will not always come from where we would like them to come from initially. For example, if you do something for somebody and they take it for granted do not get mad that they did not appreciate your service or gift. That is a battle that they will have to take up with nature, but don't let their battle make you cold from giving again. Life remains reflective, and does to you what you do to it. Good things do not always come right away, because they must be consistent acts, and negative encounters will be test. It took me four years to get me to where I am now, and it took a humbled attitude in highs and an enduring one through the lows. When someone gives you a hard time, understand what they are doing to you, they are doing to themselves. *Going the extra mile* is simply another word for the golden rule. The rule does not say to do to someone what they did to you, because you felt they deserved it. It states to do onto someone what you would like to be done onto you, because it is right. The worth you put in your work will always be in direct proportion to the compensation you receive. Time may vary in when it comes, but in time it is always sure to come.

Brandon Tyus | Bio

Brandon Tyus is rising-star in the self-improvement industry. He is building his brand as a thought developer as he believes penetrating thoughts will help uncover people's purpose.

Abandoning the streets of poverty, he has grown bigger than his problems, and has taken his experiences and equipped himself with the tools to help other people.

Brandon is currently studying to be a Napoleon Hill Foundation Certified Instructor. Through his journey, he has helped a wide range of people from college students, to car salesman, and even a CEO at a financial institution.

Brandon is ahead of his time, but knows full well that he must focus on what he can take advantage of now to build the necessary creditability to give people the sense of security they yearn for when it comes to assisting them with their purpose.

Napoleon Hill Bio

NAPOLEON HILL
(1883-1970)

*"Whatever your mind can conceive and
believe it can achieve."*

— Napoleon Hill

American born Napoleon Hill is considered to have influenced more people into success than any other person in history. He has been perhaps the most influential man in the area of personal success technique development, primarily through his classic book Think and Grow Rich which has helped million of the people and has been important in the life of many successful people such as W. Clement Stone and Og Mandino.

Napoleon Hill was born into poverty in 1883 in a one-room cabin on the Pound River in Wise County, Virginia. At the age of 10 his mother died, and two years later his father remarried. He became a very rebellious boy, but grew up to be an incredible man. He began his writing career at age 13 as a "mountain reporter" for small town newspapers and went on to become America's most beloved motivational author. Fighting against all class of great disadvantages and pressures, he dedicated more than 25 years of his life to define the reasons by which so many people fail to achieve true financial success and happiness in their life.

During this time he achieved great success as an attorney and journalist. His early career as a reporter helped finance his way through law school. He was given an assignment to write a series of success stories of famous men, and his big break came when he was asked to interview steel-magnate Andrew Carnegie. Mr. Carnegie commissioned Hill to interview over 500 millionaires to find a success formula that could be used by the average person. These included Thomas Edison, Alexander Graham Bell, Henry Ford, Elmer Gates, Charles M. Schwab, Theodore Roosevelt, William Wrigley Jr, John Wanamaker, William Jennings Bryan, George Eastman, Woodrow Wilson, William H. Taft, John D. Rockefeller, F. W. Woolworth, Jennings Randolph, among others.

He became an advisor to Andrew Carnegie, and with Carnegie's help he formulated a philosophy of success, drawing on the thoughts and experience of a multitude of rags-to-riches tycoons. It took Hill over 20 years to produce his book, a classic in the Personal Development field called Think and Grow Rich. This book has sold over 7 million copies and has helped thousands achieve success. The secret to success is very simple but you'll have to read the book to find out what it is!

Napoleon Hill passed away in November 1970 after a long and successful career writing, teaching, and lecturing about the principles of success. His work stands as a monument to individual achievement and is the cornerstone of modern motivation. His book, Think and Grow Rich, is the all-time best seller in the field.

The Seventeen Principles

1. **Definiteness of Purpose**
2. **Mastermind Alliance**
3. **Applied Faith**
4. **Going the Extra Mile**
5. **Pleasing Personality**
6. **Personal Initiative**
7. **Positive Mental Attitude**
8. **Enthusiasm**
9. **Self-Discipline**
10. **Accurate Thinking**
11. **Controlled Attention**
12. **Teamwork**
13. **Learning from Adversity & Defeat**
14. **Creative Vision**
15. **Maintenance of Sound Health**
16. **Budgeting Time and Money**
17. **Cosmic Habitforce**

About Tom "too tall" Cunningham

Tom "too tall" Cunningham's God-given life purpose is to encourage and inspire people to live positively with and through life's obstacles and adversities.

He does that as a Napoleon Hill Foundation Certified Instructor, Founder of Journey To Success Radio, and creator of the Amazon International #1 Bestselling series of books, Journeys To Success.

Tom has lived with Juvenile Rheumatoid Arthritis from his jaw to his toes since the age of 5, 48 years now.

During that time, he has had 4 hips, 4 knees, and 2 shoulders replaced and been hospitalized about 40 times.

Despite his physical challenges, Tom always answers AMAZING when asked how he is doing. He tells people that 80% of the time it is true and the other 20% of the time it is to remind himself that it is true.

About Brad Szollose

Brad Szollose

(pronounced zol-us)

> *"...No one knows Millennials or cross-generational management better than Brad, and it shows; our attendees are still talking about his work."*
>
> — Robbins Research International, Inc., a Tony Robbins Company

TEDx Speaker, award-winning business author and Web Pioneer Brad Szollose helps businesses and organizations dominate their industry by tapping into the treasure of a cross-generational workforce. Brad has been called The Millennial Whisperer, and his Liquid Leadership workshops show attendees how to ignite the power of their workforce and their customer base.

Brad is also a global business adviser and the foremost expert on Generational Issues and Workforce Engagement. His bestselling book, *Liquid Leadership: From Woodstock to Wikipedia*, shares Brad's journey beginning as a bootstrapped business idea in a coffee shop to C-level executive of a publicly traded company worth $26 million in just 24 short months; becoming the FIRST Internet Agency to go public in an IPO!

As a C-Suite Executive Brad applied his unique management style to a young, tech-savvy Generation X & Y Workforce producing great results; The company experienced 425% hyper-growth for 5 straight years with only 6% turnover. Brad's management model won K2 the Arthur Andersen NY Enterprise Award for Best Practices in Fostering Innovation Among Employees.

Today the world's leading business publications seek out Brad's insights on Millennials, and he has been featured in Forbes, The Huffington Post, New York Magazine, Inc., Advertising Age, The International Business Times, The Hindu Business Line and Le Journal du Dimanche to name a few, along with television, radio and podcast appearances on CBS and other media outlets.

Today Brad's programs have transformed a new generation of business leaders, helping them maximize their corporate culture, expectations, productivity, and sales growth in The Information Age.

Made in the USA
Lexington, KY
24 August 2017